PRAISE FO

As a social worker, I was immediately intrigued by *Pretty/Sick*; it tells a tragic story of untreated mental illness while honoring the life and strength of the person underneath, 'warts and all' (as Tim likes to say). When him and I first started working together, Tim had a disorganized collection of memories and the lessons that came with them, some in the form of poems, others in paragraphs. He had put everything onto those pages, and his vulnerability was inspiring. Some days were harder than others, and we were both required to disclose and discover parts of ourselves in order to make this book into what we wanted it to be. Eventually, we were able to put together one of the most meaningful and thought-provoking pieces of literature that I have ever had the pleasure of reading. *Pretty/Sick* doesn't sugarcoat a damn thing, and presents a challenge to each of its readers to *feel* something, whether it be connection, pain, or simply empathy. It is our hope that it goes beyond that, and provokes others to advocate for, or at least try to understand those labeled as 'weak', 'crazy', or 'undeserving' of help.

— HALEY CRABB, BSW

PRETTY/SICK

TIMOTHY DURNING

Foreword by
TED BENDER

ebook ISBN: 978-1-952836-04-6
print ISBN: 978-1-952836-05-3

Skyland Press
www.skylandpress.com

First Edition: July 2020
1 2 3 4 5 6 7 8 9 10

Disclaimer

This book deals with sexual assault, drug addiction and mental illness. While the author has taken great lengths to ensure the subject matter is dealt with in a compassionate and respectful manner, it may be troubling for some readers. Discretion is advised.

This work is based on a true story as such the events in this memoir are true to the best of the author's memory. Some of the incidents have been condensed and some names and identifying features have been changed to protect the identity of certain parties. The author in no way represents any company, corporation, or brand, mentioned herein. The views expressed in this memoir are solely those of the author.

I have tried to recreate events, locales and conversations from my memories of them. In order to maintain their anonymity in some instances I have changed the names of individuals and places, I may have changed some identifying characteristics and details such as physical properties, occupations and places of residence.

Dedication

Getting this out of my head, onto paper and, ultimately, into the work you are holding, nearly killed me at times. What began as a catharsis, like so many things in life, became an utterly soul shaking experience. What I didn't know then, was that it was an absolute necessity for me to have any chance of moving forward. This book is dedicated to the "botched and the bungled" Those kindred souls that have faced crushing adversity, found their way through, and made a personal decision to give it meaning, to "Origami that shit" To take the weight of the lead and turn it to gold, to live a life filled with intention.

TABLE OF CONTENTS

FOREWORD

Addiction and mental illness are ravaging our country. 2019 saw the highest ever number of overdose deaths in the United States, reaching almost 73,000 souls. Countless others overdosed and were saved by luck, the opioid antidote naloxone, or front-line caregivers. Despite all we know about these diseases, the toll it is taking continues to increase. As overdose deaths have increased over time, so too have completed suicides.

The following tale is one of sorrow, anguish, glimpses of hope, and devastation. It grips you from the beginning in its raw intensity, keeping you on the edge of your seat throughout. It is the story of the forgotten, the people of our country who are failed by the system, discarded, and left to fend for themselves. Often in mental illness, and especially in substance use disorders, we tend to blame them for all that has happened to them. We blame them for their drug use, not getting help for their mental illness, and making bad choices. The problem with this framework is that we are coming from a place of logic and sanity.

For those who suffer, their past has very little logic or sanity in it. They are often abused horribly as children, stripping away their innocence and teaching them that life is hell. They usually grow up around drug and alcohol use, and then we wonder why they end up using them as teens and adults. And honestly, who can blame them for turning to drugs and alcohol for at least temporary relief. Many people will luckily never know the horrors that they endured. Think about your own childhood. Was it happy? Were you loved and cared for? If so, good. That is the way it is supposed to be. But for countless others, this is far from their reality. Their reality may have been trying to avoid physical, emotional, or sexual abuse, trying to protect their siblings, or just making sure that they have food to eat that day.

This is where it gets worse. These kids grow up, victims, no fault of their own. Then what does society do? We blame THEM. They are no longer the victims of childhood turmoil and unspeakable abuse, but adults just making bad choices. Not individuals suffering from the debilitating hell of mental illness and substance use disorder, but as the scourge of society who need to be locked up. It is entirely backward. We need to be providing support, excellent clinical care, and promoting well-being and recovery for these weary travelers. They deserve our respect, empathy, and compassion. They are fighting a relentless disease that needs improved treatments, improved access to care, and a complete culture shift in the way we approach these ailments.

The following account embodies the fateful outcome of a lost soul stricken with trauma and disease. It opens a window that allows you to peer into this world of chaos from the comfort and safety of your favorite armchair. You will see what the "daily grind" entails while trying to remain a "successful addict." It is a non-stop, 24-hour job that focuses on the following skillset: manipulation, deceit, and complete loss of self-worth. It makes you do things you never saw yourself doing, and just when you think it can't get worse, you set a new bar. It is a dangerous world of pure hell, for which escape can seem an impossibility.

In my own career, I have learned exactly one thing, you NEVER know which patient will turn it around and get their life in order. I've seen young people who had multiple overdoses and were barely clinging to life make stunning turnarounds when I thought there was no hope. I have seen people who drank alcohol daily and to excess for decades put down the bottle and pick up their 5-year chip in an AA meeting. I have also seen those who were so motivated and positive that I thought for sure they would be the ones to make it. Many of them didn't make it.

I carry the gravity of those losses with me into everything I do in my professional career. The lesson from this is to never give up on anyone. Everyone deserves a chance at wellness. Statements like "they have to hit rock bottom first" or "they have to want it" are harmful and misleading.

One of the biggest problems with the United States' mental health care system is the fractured nature of services and the inequality of access to excellent care. Can you imagine being held against your will in an inpatient psychiatric unit for stabilization? Imagine for a moment what would have to happen for that to be your reality. Often times in this situation, you are "stabilized" and discharged with an aftercare plan. There is usually very little follow up, and people skip appointments. This puts them right back into the cycle. Continuity of care is lacking, and access to care has many barriers. We have to do more for the people of this country. We have to decriminalize addiction and treat people with this disorder as human beings, not as if they have some defect in moral character. Addiction is a disease. The sooner we can wrap our heads around that, the better.

Dr. Ted Bender, MBA, Ph.D., LCDC

Dr. Ted Bender is the President of UnityPoint Health – UnityPlace in Peoria, Illinois. He has a Ph.D. in clinical psychology from the Florida State University and an MBA from Texas A&M. He has been working in the field of mental health and substance use disorders for the past 15 years.

PREFACE

My name is Tim.

I am not a movie star or singer. I'm not some famous athlete. But then again, this isn't about that, nor is it about some magical journey into enlightenment. This is more about how life shows up and how we, in turn, show up for life.

There's a million *ME's* out there, a million stories. For the most part, Our stories will never be heard. No one really cares. This is a tragedy, for within Our stories lie an amalgam of life far more significant than any individual. Our collective lives and dies anonymously, yet Our experiences are the things of which all lives are made. In sharing Our stories, honestly, fearlessly, we can help to reshape our entire world. We can show the world that the universe wastes nothing. In sharing Our success, Our failure, Our everyday mundane shit, We tug away at the masks, We reveal just how much We all have in common, how similar We are in all walks of life. None of Us are terminally unique. None of Us are alone.

When I began writing, I was in deep pain. My writing was purely a catharsis to help me cope with a tragedy. It was literary vomit. I spewed my pain and my hurt upon the pages whenever I needed, anywhere, anytime. It made no difference. I simply had to get it out. While I had always had a knack for expressing myself in the written word, it was nothing more than an oddity to others, a parlor trick - that a big meathead could actually write and form words, much less that I might actually have feelings and an ability to express lucid thought beyond the realm of the weight room.

As I wrote, my work became to me as the fool to the wounded king in the story of the *Fisher King*. The words, the pages, unknowingly offering to me the grail with which to heal my pain. Unaware of my journey, the places I had been, only knowing I was thirsty.

I shared some of my work, raw as it was, and people felt it. This gave me hope. To me, this meant that the things I went through- the loss, the pain- if I could share those, and through sharing evoke those feelings in others, perhaps I had given it all reason. To lessen another's pain. To let them know that none of us are as alone or as different as we believe ourselves to be.

BEAUTY AND THE BEAST

Music has always had a huge influence on me. It seemed only appropriate to include songs that were part of this journey. This is one to take in before you start. I love the entire soundtrack. Lyrically this has always stirred my emotions. Though we evolve, we carry all the parts we have ever played. Most of us have been both roles at some point.

Beauty and the Beast
Paul Williams

This story needs to be told. I guess since I'm the other half of the story, I'm the one to tell it. Trust me, I did not want the job but, I don't take the responsibility lightly, so here I am, even though I know how fucked up this is all going to sound. To do it right, to do her right, it has to be real, warts and all. That's the only way it can be, the only way she would want it. I have to keep it 100, no, 1000, gotta keep it 1000.

That's what she always said, "100 ain't good enough motherfucker, you better keep that shit 1000!"

So, again, here I am—no one special. I have not done anything that might be considered truly exceptional, certainly not anything of which you may have heard. I made my living as a chef for over thirty years. I became a bodybuilder later in life and took up personal training and coaching. I suppose it could be said that I have risen to an acceptable level of mediocrity—average Joe. You wouldn't know me if you saw me nor, to look at me, would you be able to know the story within; our story. We don't have to be famous to have a story; we just have to be willing to share it, to let those demons out, and let others decide just what it means to them.

Please don't get the idea that this is some kind of happy ending bullshit or inspirational story about forgiveness or redemption - trust me, it's not. It's a fucked-up story. It's about fucked-up people, doing fucked-up shit, and me?

I'm just one of those fucked-up people. So, let's level the field, straight up. I am not a good person. I can't tell that lie. As I began writing, just to get it out of my head, many times, I would pause and have to read a part over and over and think to myself, "Who IS this piece of shit!?!"

I don't even recognize the person I was, but it's still my skin. I've been in it the whole time, so, no matter where I go, there I am. So, no, I'm not a good person. At best, I'm better than I was most days, and even then, opinions vary. I've been it all, a liar, a cheater, a thief; I've done and dealt more than my fair share of drugs and alcohol. She just caught me at a moment when I had found a way to rise above some of those demons, and her? Well, I caught her in full stride, running just as fast as she could, right through the razor wire.

How did we meet?

That is one of those fucked-up situations.

I was a married man, just starting a new business after a failed attempt at a restaurant. I was fighting to get it rolling. My wife, Kathy, and I were not doing well. Two damaged people. I had already had an affair, and we had separated; we would still see each other on some weekends, neither of us quite willing to just call it quits like we should have. The truth was, she wasn't happy, and I sure wasn't happy.

As had always been my MO, when I wasn't a happy camper, I sought an outside means to fix myself inside, in this case, on the street. Now, I had been clean and sober for several years at this point. While drugs and alcohol weren't part of my equation in those days, that didn't mean I was clean; I was still using. Street girls were my DOC. Street girls, hookers, that was my drug of choice. I mean, whatever it is you use to change the way you feel, that's your drug. Either an outside means; alcohol, cocaine, crack or inside, getting high on your own, dopamine, adrenaline, endorphins, we all carry our supply own as well. It was easy, $20 here, $30 there, blow jobs in parking lots, sex in your car or a shitty hotel room, just getting my fix. I saw nothing wrong with it. Damn skippy better than what I was doing just a few years earlier. At least that is how I justified it. For me, it was just another weekday. Sick, I mean legit, I did not see anything wrong with it; that was the scariest part, the lack of a moral compass, not recognizing my part, taking no ownership. They got what they wanted, I got what I wanted, no harm, no foul, a "victimless" crime.

Keeping in mind, I was still MARRIED, still seeing my wife, hell, she and I even had a great sex life, but, for me, it wasn't enough. I just wanted something more. That outside means to make myself feel better inside- I don't know, to this day, I can't really explain it, suffice it to say, addict stuff. As far as Kathy and I went, at one point, we really had a lot going for us. I would offer, somewhere along the way, we both just checked out and forgot to tell each other.

Now, on the street, generally, I would find a particular girl. One with which I could work, develop a bit of a business relationship, and then keep coming back. I didn't care for surprises; it was more comfortable for me that way. I was cruising D block (A small drug area, where most of the streets start with a D) looking for my newest girl, Sunshine; young girl, she couldn't have been more than twenty years old, but there she was, out in the meat grinder, with shitty people like me looking to play for pay. She was nowhere to be found that day, so I tried over at one of the cheap hotels that I had grown to know and love so much, to see if she may have gotten a room. Most all of the girls had drug problems; when they could manage it, they would get a room and turn tricks all day so they could smoke rock all night. The Collegiate was kicking, dope boys all over, but still no Sunshine.

I took a chance, and I slowed down to ask if any of them had seen her. Of course, you slow down to talk to a dope boy, and you're going to get five of them in your window, each with a handful of crack. If you happen to be a recovering addict, with crack being one of your DOC's, handfuls of it in your car can be somewhat problematic. I asked about Sunshine, and most of them bailed- the one that stayed, obviously an entrepreneur, asked if I wanted a woman. Apparently, he was aware of the importance of multiple revenue streams. Drug dealer/pimp- ambitious- but he knew why I was there. Damn right - I was looking for a woman! Time for my fix. He told me to park and directed me to a room; I handed him $40 and walked to the door.

Funny how you never know at the time how that one action- a knock on a hotel room door, a random meeting- can affect your entire life.

I knocked on the door, she opened it, there she stood, a beer in her hand (Natty Ice no less). She opened with, "Damn you're sexy."

I smiled; she was attractive. That "different" kind of attractive, the kind that keeps you looking but you can't quite put your finger on. She was exotic, curly dark hair, dark eyes, thin, but not a heroin chic kind of thin, more of an athletic kind of thin. She wasn't what I had expected; a bit older, several tats, no boobs. Not my usual by any means, low, raspy kind of voice. She had a sly little smile, she rubbed my chest and arms, and smirked, "This is gonna be fun!"

My guard was up, new girl and all, but she stayed warm and inviting, which made me nervous. Most first times with a new girl can be a bit cold, mechanical. She wasn't about that. She took the lead, "Take your clothes off."

Why not? I mean, that's why I was there. I dropped my shirt, she rubbed my chest again, "Mmmm muscles! God damn, you're hot!!"

She slammed her beer like she was in a race and was out of her clothes in a split second, then, out of the blue, did a handstand against the wall. It was as if she had been freed from the prison of her clothing! Random and unpredictable, she was that from the start and stayed true to form.

Introductions were due, so she asked, "What's your name, honey?"

"I'm Tim, what's yours?"

"Jessica."

Jessica...

Her name was Jessica. I had no idea at that moment how sacred that name would become; I still speak it in hushed tones.

We got in bed, and she immediately climbed on top, boom, inside, no condom, nothing, just boom. Jessica was very vocal, she knew how to play it, she was even kind enough to fake an orgasm for me. Most street girls don't give a shit about such amenities, just get your nut and get the fuck out, but Jessica was a lot different from the norm. We finished up, and she laid her head on my chest and asked softly if she could see me again. I said, of course, she got up, lit up a cigarette, and started another beer, I put my clothes back on, and she gave me her number. Business completed, off I went; she gave me a little "bye sexy" as she closed the door, again, flashing that slick little smile. I don't know what it was exactly, but somehow, transactional as it was, I felt we had clicked. Well, as much as you can click under those circumstances, but it had been different somehow, not the norm anyway. Now, Jess was *GREAT* at manipulating people, working them, and making them feel special; it was one of many gifts she had. So, that might have just been her play, but either way, she had caught my attention.

Much later, I discovered that she was at that particular hotel that day because she had recently gotten out of prison- assault and battery on a LEO- did two years of a five-year sentence, out for good behavior. Good behavior? That's a laugh, Jess and good behavior were generally mutually exclusive. The guy she was seeing at the time was acting as her pimp so she could get some paper together. Her biological mother, Annie, had just been in town to pick her up when she had gotten out. When Jess was born, Annie was forced by her father to give Jess up for adoption. Annie had not been a part of Jessica's life until her adopted family contacted her several years earlier to ask for her help. Jess had a multitude of emotional issues throughout her youth, and her adopted family was desperate for any help they could get. Annie was incredible, doing her best to become a part of Jessica's life; but of course, Jess would have had to be a willing participant for that to work. She was not. Jessica held too much resentment because of the adoption. She wasn't willing, not at all. She accepted Annie's help when offered, guilting Annie the whole time, but that was about all.

Annie and I have since become friends along this journey. We did know of each other along the way, but only what Jessica wanted us to know about each other, and there was absolutely no way she would let us speak to each other. Jess was a master at compartmentalizing relationships and manipulating how people viewed each other even though they had never met. She hated it when people would talk about her when she was not present; she was practically neurotic about it.

Annie related to me how she had come to pick up Jess from prison and that, almost immediately, Jess was back at it, having Annie drive her around to all her "friends." Introducing her and, though Annie hadn't seen it outright, she believed Jess was getting drugs as well (I'll guarantee that she was). Throughout the day, Jess had gotten completely wasted to the point where she even suggested that she and Annie do a mother/ daughter trick for some quick cash. Shocked by the invitation, it goes without saying, Annie declined and decided to return home.

With her only means of support gone, she fell in with this entrepreneur and ended up at the hotel where she and I met.

Jess and I saw each other several more times in that first year. She would mainly call me when she needed money after she had dropped her business partner. She knew I went to work at 3:30am, so, invariably, I would get calls around that time, and we would rendezvous, mainly around Charlotte street, where she stayed most of the time. Jessica didn't have an actual residence in the years I knew her- well, maybe that's not entirely true. Occasionally she would find a spot for a week or two, but mostly she would bounce from house to house, couch to couch, bed to bed.

She had a habit of convincing people to ask her to leave. It was almost a gift. At first glance, Jessica could be the life of the party, a genuinely free-spirited, fun person. But there were two sides to that coin, out of nowhere she would turn, dark, just straight up mean, no other way to put it; when she "clicked," no one wanted to be around her. Time after time, I would see people party with her, see that fun side, then out of nowhere, that beast would unleash.

Once people got a taste of that, she didn't stick around long, although, usually, it was far too late. When she clicked, there were huge scenes, broken shit, big fights, and police lights. "Crazy Jessica" was what many people came to know her as. I should have figured something was going on but, I was so self-centered, I could only see what I wanted. I would pick her up, she would have her arm bandaged, stitches in her head, limping, always a new battle wound; bug bites, infections, the signs were always there, I was simply blind, couldn't see all that was going on.

I found out quickly that Jessica did not like to be alone, even if only on the phone. She would call and talk for as long as you would let her; it was amazing. Occasionally we would have conversations, but mostly she would just start talking, nonstop, and I would sit and listen, you know, know your role/play your part, generally, I was the audience.

We got into an argument once; she was on a roll, and me, tired of hearing the bullshit, tossed my phone in a pile of clothes. After about twenty minutes, I had finished doing whatever I was doing, and I looked for my phone. I could hear her still talking. When I picked it up, sure enough, she was still going, so I said, "hello?"

She abruptly stopped, almost stunned, she slowly asked, "What?"

I explained to her I had set my phone down and she had been talking to no one, not missing a beat she said, "Well, I'ma tell you what, you missed some real good shit!!"

As my food business was growing, I ran a fairly large delivery route. Jess would often call, so I would pick her up, and she would ride along while I delivered. She didn't help, didn't even try, she would just sit there, falling asleep if it had been a long evening or chatting away if she was still going, all as I went about my work. At this point, I hadn't seen "the beast"; she generally wasn't using too much in the daytime when she would hang with me. She called me one night and wanted to see me (needed money) I told her I couldn't and -

CLICK!

She started cursing me and screaming at me, "motherfucking cracker ass cracker" (that would become one of her favorites) "get your bitch ass out here and don't bring that low ball shit, that shit is over!!"

"You gonna pay me, you fucking bitch!"

I sat there stunned, genuinely taken aback. I had never seen this side. It was pure street, straight up hood rat, it went on and on until I finally just hung up; she must have called back twenty times that night. Now, that number might sound like a lot but trust me, it wasn't, that wasn't a record, not even close- sixty-six calls in about four- hour period was her record- persistent as hell, completely fixated. A Pitbull mentality, she would not let shit go. She finally did quit calling that evening. The next morning when I got up, I was curious, curious as to just what had happened to her. I drove over to Charlotte Street. There she was, staggering down the road with something on her head, or maybe in her hair. When she first saw me, she tried to duck into some bushes. It was a half-assed attempt, and as I got closer, she stepped back out. Glaring at me. I could see what it was, a big hairpiece, like extensions, that had somehow been woven half in and half out of her hair- it was comical, she was pulling at it and trying like hell to get it out but, without cutting her hair, it wasn't going anywhere.

She got in the car, and I could immediately tell she was different- angry, mean, aggressive. Chuckling to myself, I asked what the story might be. Grudgingly she related how she had a girlfriend putting this weave in her hair when things went south. Of course, She showed her ass. So, as had always happened, they kicked said ass out and just left her to deal with it. There she sat with this thing stuck in her hair, still cursing me, still drinking, making threats, just plain nasty. Now, this had been my first time actually seeing the "beast," so I had no idea what to do or how far she could take things. Tired of the abuse, I finally asked her to get out of my car, To which I received,

"Fuck you motherfucker!! Get me out!!"

Huh??

What did she say?

"Jess, I got shit to do today, and you aren't riding with so, please, get out."

Again, she came with, "Get me the fuck out, you pussy! You must have thought it was white boy day!! I ain't going anywhere!"

I am by no means a badass, but I am a competitive bodybuilder, and it could be said I look the part. I am not a small guy. I purposefully crafted an intimidating look to keep people at arm's length.

So, here is this 150lbs woman threatening me and daring me to get her out of my fucking car. It didn't compute; I just couldn't comprehend the situation. I was weighing about 230lbs at the time, bald head, goatee, but there we were. I kept telling her to go, and she kept telling me no and daring me to do something about it.

I had never had someone challenge me like that. It was crazy.... crazy.... well, crazy was a word I truly didn't understand before Jessica. People throw that word around a lot, it's used casually, jokingly in everyday life, "he/she so crazy!" But that's not crazy- once you've seen crazy, I mean really, deep down, looked into its eyes, crazy means something very different, crazy becomes frighteningly real.

Well, I had to go, I had shit to do, work, family, training; but Jessica wouldn't budge. I continued to ask, and she continued to spew more venom. I was not about to put my hands on her, so what do you do? I did the next best thing I could think to do-

I drove her to the police department!

Now don't get it twisted. I didn't spring this on her. I didn't just drive her there and go, "now what bitch?" I told her exactly what I was doing and where I was going, but she still would not back down. I don't think anyone else she was fucking with at the time would have even thought to pull this move off. First off, most all of them were using and at least as fucked up as she was!

Secondly, my arrogance told me, I'm clean and sober, a respectable business owner; what could go wrong? I drive up with a raving lunatic in my car, boom! This was a no brainer. As loud and obnoxious as she had already been, once we got to the station she turned it up a notch, now more threatening, more directed, "I can't wait to see you get your ass beat, I'm gonna have somebody snatch your cracker ass up, you're gonna bleed motherfucker!! I can't believe nobody has whipped your ass yet!!"

She was screaming at me so hard she was literally running out of breath. As I think back, it reminded me of a child, a young one, angry, but tired, doesn't want to sleep, so they pitch a huge fit to keep themselves awake.

Now, despite all of her insults, all of her threats, I really didn't want to see her go to jail and, quite honestly, I thought she would back down once we got to the station, but in true Jessica form, she proved me wrong, yet again, and she only got worse. I warned her again and again; inside, I was churning, but outside I was laughing and cracking jokes, not helping things. So finally, I went inside and calmly explained to the officer on duty what the situation was. I thought he would just come out, tell her to get the fuck out, and that would be the end of my crazy morning.

Well, that wasn't how it worked, and he explained why. I would have had to wait for a squad car to arrive, and then she would be given her options: if she chose option "B" she would be arrested. The officer looked at me plain faced and asked, "Are you sure that's what you want? You really need to think about it."

No... I wasn't sure. I went back out to the car, and before I even got close, I could hear her screaming at the top of her lungs, her voice breaking, "Motherfucker get me the fuck out of here!! I' ma tell you some good shit, I put some shit in your car, you're gonna go to jail motherfucker!! Take me back!!"

As useless as I knew it was, I asked her if she was going to get out if I took her back and as expected I got, "Guess you'll find out bitch, you fucking cracker!!"

Well, I didn't want her in jail, so I agreed to take her back. She was still calling me everything but a Christian, but still, she never laid a hand on me. I would find out later, that was telling. Jessica fought anybody about anything for any reason. She wasn't afraid to lay hands on people, but that day, for some reason, she never touched me. I can only assume it was my size, I was a lot bigger, and while she may not have been able to shut her mouth to save her life, she could keep her hands to herself when she had to.

As we drove back to Charlotte Street, Jess started winding down, and she explained that night, her brother had called her and told her that her mother had died. I had lost my mother several years earlier, so my empathy immediately kicked in. Let me first explain, Jessica had two mothers, her biological mother Annie, whom I mentioned earlier, and her adopted mother, Missy Lynn.

The story (as Jess told it) was that her birth mother, Annie, was a heroin addict, and while Annie was pregnant with Jessica, she had attempted suicide. The stress affected Jess long before she was ever born. Jess explained to me that she was who she was because of that singular event, further, that the world, as we know it, is composed of light and dark. Both are needed, both integral parts of this world. That was why she was the way she was; she was the dark, she called herself that, the dark. She believed herself the antithesis, the yang in the world—a dark muse. Jessica donned the frowning mask of Melpomene, and she martyred herself time and time again in accepting her role.

Missy Lynn was Jessica's adopted mother. Jessica couldn't even say Missy Lynn's name without over-emphasizing it. She couldn't stand Missy Lynn. She spat her name with contempt every time she spoke it, but Missy Lynn was still her mother, and finding out that she had passed was a shock to her. I found out a little later than her brother had either lied, or she fabricated the whole thing, as her mother had not, in fact, died. Years later, I also was to learn that Annie was NOT a heroin addict. Just made for a good narrative for Jess to explain the things about herself that she couldn't understand. As she spoke about her estranged relationship with her adopted mother, I would try to comfort her, but if I so much as touched her, she would bristle, and shoot a,

"I' ma tell you some good shit, you like that hand? You best move it!"

She was still winding down, so I pulled up to Mr. Davis's. Mr. Davis was an older gentleman (a letch) who had a house on Charlotte St. Mr. Davis would let some of the street girls stay with him for certain favors. Jessica, however, was not allowed to stay in the house. Mr. Davis was intimidated by her, with good reason; Jess didn't take kindly to his advances toward her or her "friends", and she certainly didn't like being taken advantage of, nor was she afraid to tell you. So, Mr. Davis was kind enough to make other arrangements for Jess. She stayed outside in the cab of his truck. He gave her a blanket, and that's where she would spend her night, whatever the weather, even in the freezing cold, there she stayed. I had learned this when I came to get her one morning in thirty-degree weather and watched as she unfolded herself out of the truck.

Later I began to really understand just how sad all this was, for her to be so isolated, unwanted, so all alone, alone with her thoughts, thoughts of her kids, her mothers, her family, her life. Thoughts undoubtedly twisted from that isolation. She was utterly desolate. It was so tragic, but as I was to discover tragedy was nothing new to Jess, it was her life.

A sea of chaos.

And Jessica?

I learned quickly…

Jessica truly was tragedy's muse.

DRIVE

In the first year we met, a call from the Budget Inn led to one of our first "Come get me" scenarios. Jess had a room, nothing unusual there, but as this was early on for us, I didn't quite grasp the dynamic; A room meant business of one kind or another. She called me and begged me to come and talk to the cops for her. As became my MO, I headed over. I arrived to the sight of two cop cars, with Jess bloodied and screaming at the door to her room. I parked and headed toward her. Tallahassee's finest stopped me and asked if I knew her. I said yes, she was a friend. Uh-huh, A friend, right, I might as well have said I was her dad; they might have believed that more.

Anyway, they explained they had been called by the motel because she was creating a public disturbance. All they'd got so far is that she had been in a fight and looked like she had taken a solid beating. I asked with whom she had been fighting, and they explained that's what they were trying to find out, but she wasn't exactly cooperating. They were willing to let me handle it if I promised I could calm her down and that if she wanted to, she could file a complaint the next day. I said I would handle it. The boys in blue seemed relieved and bailed as quickly as a fish throws a hook.

I walked in the room- she was laying on the bed, face down with her face in a bloody towel- I said, "Jess, you ok?"

She sat up and took the towel off her face. It was painfully obvious that her nose was broken and pushed to one side of her face. "Does it look like I'm ok, Motherfucker?"

Holy Shit!! Her face was a bloody mess, eye swollen, her nose was, well, it was grotesque. I told her, "You look like you need an ambulance."

To which I got, "I already said no to that, dumb-ass. Why do you think I'm still here? Stupid ass cracker...."

It was in these moments when I would begin to ask myself.... why the fuck am I here again??

I go out of my way to come help only to get called a dumbass. On second thought, I had volunteered for this duty, so maybe she had a point. Either way, I attempted compassion.

"I'm so sorry this happened babe, who did this to you?"

She explained, "Motherfucking dope boy, was supposed to give me some dope for helping him, but changed his mind, I tried to snatch his chain, and he sucker-punched me."

I did not know at this point just how adept Jess was at fighting. Had I known then what I know now, I would have been feeling sorry for him. Instead, I was pissed off at this punk who would lay hands on her. In retrospect, I'm sure he got at least as good as he gave, which is probably why he vanished.

I told her I wanted to help; she was less than grateful but halfheart-edly complied. I took her to the bathroom and washed her face and hands. I had no idea what to do about the nose. It was just, well, it was just fucked up. I said she needed a doctor, to which she answered, and I quote), "Fuck that!! Just set it straight."

Plain faced I blinked and with a slight shake of my head responded "What? I'm sorry, what did you say?"

She repeated, "You can set it, it's not that fucking hard, don't be a fucking pussy."

I was sick to my stomach and still baffled by her request. "You seriously want ME to set your nose?"

Yet again, she said it, with more colorful metaphors sprinkled in at my expense.

After all the abuse I had taken from her, I should have been happy to set it, just to even the score; but, ugh, move her broken nose back in place? With my hands...?

Well, her patience was done, so she gave me the: "How to set a broken nose for dummies" speech, and for some insane reason I could never explain, I agreed.

I placed my hands on either side of her head, held the bridge of her nose between my thumbs, and said, "on the count of three...one, two, three!!"

I shifted the bone back to center, and, almost like a jigsaw puzzle piece, it crunched into place. She screamed a brief stream of obscenities and settled right back down.

"That wasn't that fucking hard now, was it?"

I felt like I was gonna puke. It was horrible, the feel of it, the sound, horrible. But it was back where it belonged; and, as sick as it made me feel, I was also feeling like a white knight. Unfortunately, she was not feeling the whole "white knight" vibe. Getting her nose back where it belonged did nothing for her disposition. If anything, she was meaner.

"Give me some fucking money, motherfucker, I need a drink."

I started to tally it up: kept her away from the cops, cleaned her up, fixed her nose, by my account, I had completed my duties here. I told her no and that I was heading home. That wasn't part of her agenda, "Oh, you just gonna leave my ass here all alone, no money, no food, nothing to drink...?"

16

sgh.

Wait, let me think for a minute, umm, YES!! That was exactly my plan, I had already done more than I should have, I knew I wasn't getting laid (nor did I want to), I was tired of being cursed, I was done.

"Girl, I got to go, this has already taken too much time, and I'm tired of getting bitched at. I got shit to do, I'm out."

She was tired, emotionally, physically, but she had just enough to give me a glimpse into our future, "Ok, ok, go motherfucker!! Go!! But don't you call me again and damn sure don't let me see your cracker ass down here again. I will fucking KILL you!! You hear me bitch? I will fucking end your white ass, piece-o-shit motherfucker, dead!!"

I was in my car and gone before she even finished, she had followed me out into the parking lot, I could hear her still going off, "you're a dead fucking cracker, you just don't know it!"

I do not believe I had ever had someone say they were going to kill me previous to that, at least not seriously, maybe as a joke, but never like that, with malice, with intent. There are certain truths that as we develop into adults we MUST learn. Ignoring these truths can leave us wide open to some nasty shit, vulnerable. This was one of those truths.

Maya Angelou was a speaker of truths and presented them incredibly eloquently: "*When someone shows you who they truly are for the first time, believe them.*"

Truth, 1000!!! Today I fully embrace the concept that if someone threatens your life, for real. That's the end. There is no going back. If they said and if they meant it, it is permanent, no take-backs, no do-overs; that, my friends, is a wrap, check, please.

Once we had started to settle in a little more, we also began to explore some of our relationship's more exciting dynamics. One of Jessica's favorite past times became calling me and keeping me on the line while she was on maneuvers. She would call from a hotel room or dope house while she was dealing crack or meth, I would sit there and listen to her badass self as she directed traffic, "Where's that flow? There you go, move it, no flow, got to go. Don't try me bitch, get the fuck outta here!!"

I heard the transactions as each went down. Jess had a well-deserved rep for being a badass, she had no fear, didn't take shit from anybody, and that mouth? Oh my God, that mouth would let you know where you stood real quick. Because of that, several of the dope boys along the way would trade with her to help move product and keep things in order, dope for her services.

One afternoon she called from a motel, a run-down roach and bed bug-infested property on the way out of town. She was already in a conversation but wasn't speaking to me, I could hear her talking to someone in the room with a calm, but serious voice, I heard some commotion going on, but Jess just kept her voice down as she told the person some good shit,

"Calm down bitch, don't be stupid, put that shit down..."

BOOM!!

Suddenly everything erupted. I could hear screaming, furniture moving, and a huge fight. I kept yelling for Jess, but she wouldn't answer; I hung up. It was too intense, the shit tightened up my inside. Sure enough, 5 minutes later Jess called back, screaming, crying, "You gotta come to get me, PLEASE come get me, OH MY GOD!! PLEASE!!" What the FUCK?!?!

I wasn't far from the motel, so I raced over. As I drove into the parking lot, my head was spinning, I was expecting to see, I don't know, SOMETHING? Instead, nothing, no, Jess, no cops, no commotion, nothing. Did I have the wrong motel? I looked down the road and saw her staggering down the sidewalk- I drove to her, her face was covered in blood, and she had a substantial V-shaped gash right in the center of her forehead.

I kept asking her what happened, but she wasn't really lucid, she was in a panic, maybe in shock, muttering to herself, "Oh Goddamn, I fucked up now. What am I gonna do? OH MY GOD!! WHAT THE FUCK AM I GUNNA DO!! I gotta go, you gotta get me a bus ticket, I gotta get out of town!!"

This was real. This wasn't some bullshit where she was trying to garner sympathy or get some paper. Something terrible had happened, I tried to calm her down. I just kept talking to her, to get her to tell me what had happened

"Jessica, what the fuck happened?? What's going on?? Talk to me, girl, what happened?"

She was still muttering to herself, getting out of town, going someplace else. I continued, "Jess, c'mon you gotta tell me what happened!!"

She finally started to come back, relating what had happened. "Had that bitch in a headlock."

Side Note: "headlock" = hooked someone on drugs to the point where they kept spending all their money...

Jess continued. "She was spending, but she ran out of money, she'd said she had some more on the way, so I fronted her some, but when I asked where the cash was, she couldn't come up with it. She still wanted more, but I said fuck that! She started threatening me, grabbed an ashtray, hit me in the head."

This just sounded like Tuesday for Jess. I had heard these stories from the start. I continued trying to find out where the "bad" was.

"So, are you ok?? Where is the girl?"

The way Jess had bolted from the room was odd; I couldn't figure out what else had happened. She stammered out, "She hit me, I was bleeding, I pulled out my knife, showed it to the bitch, I SHOWED IT TO HER, but she kept on. She ducked down to grab my legs, so I stabbed her, I fucking stabbed that bitch!!"

Huh?? What the fuck? Not quite believing what I had heard, I asked, "You.....you fucking stabbed her?? Is she ok?? What the fuck, Jessica?"

She snapped back, "I told you I pulled out my knife and stabbed her. I stabbed her right in her fucking neck!"

Now reality punched me right in the mouth, "Are you fucking serious Jessica, you fucking stabbed her?? Did you kill her? You didn't kill her, did you??"

She said she didn't know that the girl was still moving, still screaming when she left.

Great. Now she had made me an accessory to some fucked up charge, and *SHE FUCKING STABBED SOMEBODY*!! Ok, so now, TV shows, Movies all the shit I had seen in fiction raced through my head, I came with, "Where's your knife, Jess? You got to get rid of that fucking knife, get that fucking knife out of my car."

She spat out, "I don't have it, I don't have it!!"

She didn't have it. She didn't fucking have it?!?!

Relatively matter of factly, considering the situation, I calmly asked, "You just stabbed someone....in the fucking neck... and now you can't find your knife??"

Panicked, she shouted, "It's in the room, still in the room, I stabbed her so hard it stuck, I couldn't pull it out, it stuck in her neck, I felt it hit the bone, when I tried to pull it out it wouldn't come, it was stuck!!"

My mind was racing. I had NO idea what to do; the learning curve on this shit was beyond ridiculous.

I took her to another hotel on the opposite side of town, pulled out my handy first aid kit (I kept one in my car for the longest time and had never used it until that day), I got her all cleaned up. She needed stitches, but I didn't think the hospital was a great idea, so I butterflied it as best I could. She was calming down now, but this was heavy; this shit just hung over the room. All we really knew to do was to sit tight and wait it out.

We never heard it on the news. Apparently, no cops were called. Jess made a few calls. The girl was ok; she had a friend get her to the hospital. Would have loved to have heard the explanation for the big buck knife sticking out of her neck. Jess hadn't hit any major nerves or vessels; it was amazingly lucky.

Weeks later Jess told me she saw the girl back out on the street and couldn't help but brag on how she had fucked her up, "See what happens when you fuck with me?"-type stuff, I wasn't there to see it. Still, as she relayed it to me, all I could do was flash back to her voice's fear. In her eyes, directly following the incident and how she had now brushed it off and turned it in her favor.

What was becoming more and more evident was how I was now changing, these insane incidents simply melding in as part of my life. Something I learned from my time with Jessica was that, simply put, mental illness is contagious. It not only affects the individual, but it also affects anyone who gets too close, like a fucking virus. The first time you see that craziness, that insanity it repels you, makes you shake, tightens your stomach. But each successive time it affects you a little less, each and every time you become more and more desensitized, conditioned. Until one day, when something big happens, it's just Tuesday. It is who you are. It has become what the French call Follie Au Deux: "A shared madness." My relationship with Jess was changing me, and not for the better. Just how far it had gone was yet to be seen.

Jumping ahead a bit, around a year and a half, two years. We were seeing each other regularly but hadn't quite crossed the line into "couple." She called me for a ride late one night, 1 AM; I knew what was up, knew she was fucked up, and had shown her ass somewhere and been "requested" to leave. I told her no fucking way.

Now by this time, I was well aware that Jessica late night was a losing proposition. She kept calling, begging me to come to get her; I knew this would continue, so I asked her if she had a place to stay, and she said she did, she just needed a ride.

Very reluctantly, I agreed. When I got there, she was outside in the yard, yelling at the people in the house, "Come fuck with me now bitches, I got my man now. He'll fuck you up!!"

Jess loved to use my size and intimidating appearance to her advantage, to her and anybody else, I was her man, jacked up on steroids and jealous AF. At any moment, I could kick in a motel room door, lay waste to everybody in there, and whisk my girl away to safety.

None of these things had ever transpired, but it made a decent threat when she needed it. I met several of her acquaintances who, after meeting me, (the ones who would actually speak), would tell me that "you're not at all what I expected. Jessica always said you were crazy, all "jacked up on steroids" and really overly protective of her." It explained a lot, as most times when I would meet her peeps, they wouldn't talk, hands in laps, nervous; it seemed my reputation had preceded me. Well, Jessica's version of me. But eventually, I played into it. For reasons yet to be revealed, I had crafted this intimidating look to keep people at a safe distance. I enjoyed playing Jessica's version of me from time to time. It was flattering, and everybody loves to have their ego stroked. As I played the role, we were this fucked up power couple. I was buying into her imagination, her delusion; somehow, it was becoming our reality.

So, I picked her up and asked where we were going. Her directions were awfully close to my house, just off Pullen Rd. She kept telling me I should just let her stay with me, but I made it clear that it wouldn't happen. Too many times I had dealt with that late-night, fucked up Jess. She was not happy. I could see her starting to turn. She had me drive around Pullen Rd for thirty minutes, figuring out which house it was. Yes, I was that dumb. I claim fatigue, but eventually, I figured out it was just a Jessica ploy to get in my car. I started getting pissed, almost 2 AM driving around with a drunken time bomb. I told her I was taking her back to where I got her from,

"Fuck no, you ain't, just take me to your house, I promise I'll behave..."

Uh, yeah, I was quickly having a case of Deja Vu -I had heard that shit before. I snapped at her, "No fucking way, Jessica, you told me you had a place to stay, what the fuck?"

I spat at my windshield, a bad habit I still have today- when I get overly angry, I spit- attractive, I know. She knew of this lovely trait and decided to jump on that wagon. She spit on my cheek. I sat there, trying to process what had just happened. Did she just spit on me? Not being one to shy from a challenge, I spit back in her face. We spent the next couple minutes going back and forth... back and forth... spitting... on each other...

After putting this down on paper, I sat and read it over and over and over again.

What the fuck? Two grown-ass people.....GROWN ASS PEOPLE?!?!?!

The fit subsided, and we sat quietly for a moment, looked up at each other, and laughed. A microcosm for the "us" we were creating. A relationship so far gone from the real world that, in it, this sick-ass incident was actually funny to us in our own little reality. She spoke first, trying to play it off

"Baby, you need to take me home, your home!"

She was her coy little self, throwing that sexy little sideways glance, and honestly, at that point, I considered it but; Late night—drunk Jess. No way. I still wasn't going to chance it, "No babe, I can't do it. I'll take you back where I picked you up."

CLICK.

"Fuck you, then motherfucker! You fuckin cracker-ass cracker! You all up on that fuck shit, you think you're so much better than I am mother fucker!!"

She was all in my face, spit flying as she was screaming. Now, I could feel anger, real, profound anger building up inside. Anger at her for yet again lying to me, at myself for knowing better and still putting myself in this position.

I glared at her and shouted, "FUCK YOU, JESS!! I'm taking you back!!"

Pullen Rd is a narrow road with very deep ditches on one side- I didn't notice. Still, Jess had planted her feet on the car door. The minute I turned my gaze back to the road, she launched herself off the passenger side door and hit me in the side of the head with her forearm and elbow. I never saw it coming -she hit me like a baseball bat!

My head bounced off the driver's side window!! I NEVER would have expected to be hit THAT hard, in THAT small a space by anyone, let alone by a woman. She grabbed the wheel and tried to turn the vehicle into the ditch. I was disoriented at first, just trying to get her off the wheel, trying to stay on the road. I would push her off, and she would jump right back on again. She was full-blown activated, and I had put myself in a very, very bad position. I finally held her off with my right arm, trying to hold her in place, in desperation, but she was having nothing to do with it. Suddenly, my desperation turned to something else.

I had had enough.

Now I clicked.

I pushed her back into her seat and brought my arm back across my body. As she tried to sit back up, I swung a hard hammer fist right into her mouth, splitting her lip. She was stunned, hell, I was stunned. I took that time to pull into an apartment complex's driveway. Yelling at her now, "You better calm the fuck down, Jess!! I am not playing with you anymore!!"

Back she came punching, scratching, anything she could do, she was like a feral cat, but I was done, over the top done. I grabbed her by her face with both hands. I slammed her head against the passenger door. In the process, my thumb went into the inside corner of her eye. Right beside the bridge of her nose, up to the knuckle. I slammed her head against the door a couple times to make sure she heard me.

"YOU ARE NOT IN CHARGE HERE ANYMORE BITCH! YOU HEAR ME? Now you WILL calm the fuck down, or I will pop that fucking eye right out of your fucking head!!"

WHAT?!?!

Who the fuck just said that!?!

Was that me?

She was crying, pinned against the door, I told her I'd let her go if she calmed down, she was in shock at the ferocity with which I came at her. Truth is, so was I. I had put up with so much, for so long: the name-calling, the threats, the downright bullying, and just taken it and taken it and taken it, that anger was pent up deep inside me, until that moment, now it was my turn, now I was done, perhaps undone.

I released her, and she quickly opened the door and scurried like a wounded animal on to the ground outside. She was bawling, "How could you do this?? how could you do this?? What the fuck?? Look how much bigger you are than me, oh my god...OH MY GOD!!"

Her cries were high pitched squeals. She was like a little girl all of a sudden. I truly hurt for her; at that moment, I didn't know if I had done the right thing. Well, there's no fucking world where that was the right thing, but it is what happened.

I asked her, "What the fuck did you think was going to happen, Jess? You crack me upside my head, try to wreck my fucking car, are you fucking crazy?!?! God damn it, girl!! What the fuck was I supposed to do??"

She snapped back, "You could have warned me!! Should have warned me!! Should have said 'Imma tell you some good shit!!' You sucker-punched me, you fucking bitch!!"

I got out to help her, she was still scared and scooted away. I told her I was so sorry and finally was able to hold her. I got her back in the car and took a look at the damage to her eye. It was completely blood red and swollen shut, but the cornea wasn't scratched nor punctured. Her lip was split, bleeding, swollen. Look at what I did. I kept repeating to myself, look at what you did, you fucking asshole!! While I saw it and told myself these things, I hadn't really processed it yet. Guilt, shame, the whole gambit they should have been there, but I was numb in that moment, I wasn't feeling, only thinking, reacting. I took her to a gas station to clean her up some. But as we pulled up, she leaned out the car at a couple walking in the parking lot and said, "Look what this mother-fucker did to me, he beat my ass because I yelled at him."

The girl gave me her best stink-eye and said, "You need an ass-kick-ing, you fucking pussy ass bitch!!"

Her man hardly picked his head up. He wasn't interested. I started to explain more but immediately stopped. Who really gave a fuck?? These two weren't about to do anything, and explaining anything was just a waste of my time. I took her to a hotel to treat her. Her eye was very swollen and still blood red. I washed her off and iced it down. I had seen her in worse shape than this, much worse, but never at my hands.

We didn't talk much, each of us trapped in our own minds, review-ing, reliving, it was an uncomfortable silence. I asked if she was hungry and went to a convenience store to get some food and a Natty Ice so she wouldn't have to worry about withdrawals. She was exhausted, and I was emotionally spent. I had been in fights before but never had I come unglued like that. It was significantly less like me and very more like Jessica. Again, Follie au Deux, I was becoming more like Jess in that sense, the click, that loss of control, losing it. Here's the fucked part; it felt good. Going back to that addict thing, that rush of adrenaline, getting high on your own supply.

As a postscript to what I mentioned previously – about mental illness being contagious – I have since determined that not only is it contagious, but, as it pertains to relationships, it is also sexually transmitted. I don't believe you can be involved with someone who has an untreated mental illness and not be affected; it's simply not realistic. Reality is what you see every day. This was becoming my reality.

BRING ME TO LIFE

That moment your soul reacts to another's energy.
Starting long frozen wheels turning again. I would
listen after you read
Bring me to life
Evanescence

My son, trying his best to avoid a beating for getting high, yet again, and, being the incredibly resourceful young man he was, played the "I think I might be gay" card. I am not actually sure that is a thing, but he did it and pulled it off. THAT is an interesting position to be in as a parent. No, I wasn't happy with his choices as far as pot went (keep in mind I was in recovery); but also, if he was telling the truth, I couldn't freak out. To be real, I was actually pretty collected about it. I had many gay friends, so it really wasn't that big a deal to me. That is not to say it didn't cross my mind or weigh on me a little. Jess picked up on that quickly.

"What the fuck's up with you, somebody kill your dog?"

She was being cute. We still didn't know each other that well, but for some reason, I felt comfortable confiding in her that day. Maybe because who the hell was she going to tell anyway? Or maybe because I run my mouth a lot more than I should about just about anything going on in my life.

I don't know, but it was on my mind, so I shared it with her, "Well, I busted my boy for smoking pot again, and in our discussion, he confided in me that he thinks he might be gay."

She sat stunned for a moment, "You better be careful how you play that one. My mom lost her shit when we had that talk, that's one of the triggers that put me out here."

Somehow, I was something different in her mind. I told her, "I know Jess, I got this. I didn't freak out, just told him it didn't matter, he's my son, I love him no matter what."

Now she was really stunned, her eyes welled up. She started to quietly ramble a bit, "Now that's my mutha fuckin' dog right there, that's the shit, Fuck yeah! Mad props to you, that's the right thing to do. My mom hated that shit -told me I was un-natural, made me feel like I was a freak. You did your boy right, mad props, mad props..."

She was crying, but I wasn't sure exactly why. I just continued to explain that it wasn't a huge deal, people get to choose who they are, and we have to learn to be ok with that.

She stopped and looked at me, with an odd look, something. I don't know, like.... gratitude?

She took a breath as if to speak, but she paused as if she wasn't sure what to say. Finally, with a distant look, she spoke. "Thank you. Ain't many real motherfuckers out here. When somebody tells me something, all they trying to do is get some dope or get a hand down my pants, nobody shares shit like that with me. They don't give a fuck about me. Since I gave my kids up, I don't hear shit like that. Nobody wants to tell me about their kids, their family, THAT, was real. I need to hear real," she trailed off, still staring somewhere far away, vacant. She finished with, "It's a fucked up crazy life out here, thank you for being real with me."

There she was.

I should have thanked her as well because that was the "realest" I had seen her. It helped me too. It altered my perspective. It was in these little moments that, from the beginning, confirmed the fact that there was more to this than either of us realized.

My business was starting to take off, so five days a week, I would be out delivering food, then on Saturday and Sunday, I attempted to collect cash from the Frat boys that purchased my food. I would hang out in the frat house parking lots and wait for them to wake up from the night's festivities. It wasn't uncommon for me to drive around with $600-$700 by Sunday. Jessica was funny around cash, she would swear to everything holy that she would never take money from anyone who trusted her, but time and time again, when she was involved, money (or drugs) would come up missing.

I, however, kept a tight rein on the business cash. She loved just to look at it, and, quite honestly, she knew she was going to get some anyway- at that time, that was just how things were between us. Getting to know her early on was spotty. We would ride for hours some days. She would just ramble on and on and on about anything that came to mind. Other days she'd be passed out in the passenger's seat. On rare occasions, she would allow me to get a word in edgewise. That was when we shared more of ourselves.

Jessica called me one day while I was running my route. It was funny because even after knowing her for a relatively short time, you could tell which Jessica you were talking to in the first minute this day. She sounded "awake," so she was "on" or activated as she liked to call it. She asked me to come to pick her up from a hotel on the outskirts of Tally. The truth was, she didn't really know where she was. She gave me an address she found on the hotel phone. Luckily my route ran me in that direction. I called when I got there and told her to come out, but instead, she asked me to come to the room.

I complied.

, Upon entering, it seemed that the room didn't really look like anyone had been there very long, the bed was made, covers hardly ruffled. I made a comment or two about how it looked like she must have just arrived, but she just blew it off. She wasn't talking. There was an open bottle of amaretto that she was still working on but no evidence of anything else, a little odd, to say the least. She told me she actually really didn't know where she was or how she got there, only that she had arrived with a couple and that they had subsequently bailed on her. Of course, me being the single-minded jack ass that I was, all I could think was, we were in this hotel room, and I had a little time to spare, so I suggested we work out a trade. Of course, Jess was always willing, so we were naked in no time. Didn't take long, and soon we were on our way out the door. As we hit the parking lot, Freddy, a longtime friend, and meth cook and dealer that Jess had stayed with, showed up. She decided to have him take her to his place, and I was fine with it, as I had more drops to make. Before she left, Jess asked if I had a couple of bucks for her, I gave her $5, cigarette money, and we parted ways.

I got a call 20 minutes later. It was Jess, "What the fuck is this? $5?"

I told her that was all I had and that I had come all the way out there to get her.

"Ok, ok, you got me cracker, you got me!"

"What the fuck!! I got you?? I drove all the way out there to get you, I'm not your fucking ATM!!"

That wasn't what she wanted to hear, we had sex, and that meant money. She was pissed, I was pissed, lots of yelling. I could hear Freddy in the background egging her on, "meat stick, meat stick" (that was my pet name when Jess was pissed off at me). When we hung up, we didn't speak for weeks.

Then one day, I got a call from an odd number. I didn't recognize it, so I let it go to voicemail. When I checked it later, I found it was a call from the county jail...

Jess had been arrested.

The next time I saw the number, I accepted it. It was indeed Jess, but her voice was shaky, very quiet, meek, VERY un-Jess like. I asked what had happened, she explained that one of her other "friends" let her drive his car; let me preface this with the fact that Jess had her license suspended, many times, so many times, in fact, that she was never getting it back, at least not in this lifetime. Why some moron would even consider letting her drive will always be a mystery to me, but he had, and Jess had rear-ended a city bus. No license, paraphernalia, prescription medication, a slew of charges, and now a stint in the county.

I had never been to a jail before, either as a resident or a guest, but Jess asked me if I would come to visit her. So, I did. I got the address and made my way there. It was located in a lovely part of town, and my mind was all over the place as I pulled in to park.

Upon walking in, it was very apparent, jail is a hard, cold place; everyone is very serious, there are no smiles, no niceties, and the front desk people treat you as if you were about to be a resident in the very near future. I signed in and made the long walk to an elevator that took me to the visiting area. Every step echoed along the way in the sterile environment- I imagined I could hear calls of "dead man walking" as I trod along.

When I reached her pod, I sat down and used the phone to call the guard station and asked to speak to Jessica. They called her name out loud, and I waited. It took a second call, but finally, she made her way to me. She walked slow, covered in a blanket; she looked horrible, pallid, shaky, her hands and body were physically shaking. She was detoxing- cold turkey- I had never seen anything like it. It was horrible. She had lost weight since I had seen her. I hated it. Hated seeing her like that. Her voice was very low and very shaky.

She was very down, very sad. She cried several times during the visit. When I asked how it all went down, she perked up a bit, to tell her side. It was all bullshit, she had a prescription, wasn't her pipe.....etc....... all her usual shit I had heard 1000 times before, but something was differ-ent, and it wasn't her story. It was something else- she was different, vulnerable, afraid. I was beginning to glimpse the real Jessica, the one of which I had only seen shadows, the one I had yet to meet.

At this point, in this place, there was a surrender to her attitude, or maybe it was a resignation, an acceptance, it was hard to put my finger on it. I came and saw her almost every day for the next 6 months; the first few days were really bad. She was so sick, her whole body shaking, everything hurt. The violence of the tremors, the dry heaves, it was frightening, almost too much so to watch.

Day by day, though, she got a little better, her confidence slowly returning, smiling more, a little more positive. We had shared some physically intimate moments in our time together, but now we were getting to know each other for real. We talked about her children, her mothers, her dreams. For the first time, there was no desire or physicality to get in the way. I liked this person; she was unique, genuine, and funny.

I saw potential.

Jessica had an incredible internal light, an innate zest for life- she was also incredibly sensitive, painfully so. She would say simply too much so for this world. She was rambling on about some of her "friends" one chat when I made an offhand comment about whether they had to pay as well. She stopped abruptly, staring at me blankly, her eyes welled up, and she started crying. She asked me how I could be so cruel, how could I, why would I say that? I immediately regretted the comment. I hadn't seen her so vulnerable, so easily hurt.

At first glance, Jess seemed quite thick-skinned, but as I got to know her, especially in this setting, I quickly realized that much of that appearance was a defense mechanism, a skill she learned to protect her heart. Make no mistake- Jess was a VERY tough individual, as tough as I've ever seen, however, because she was actually hypersensitive, when she got her feelings hurt, to keep from appearing weak or soft, she would lash out to protect herself. In this place, stripped of any trappings, unable to retaliate, or make a physical presence, she was just flat out vulnerable.

I left that day feeling like I really wanted to help this distracted soul. I saw potential, I saw possibilities, and, honestly, for the first time, I saw the person. For so long, I had always considered my actions, picking up street girls, as a victimless crime- the word exploitation never came to mind, I didn't see a daughter or a wife or a mother, I couldn't see the person who was trapped, imprisoned in this life, they were a means to an end for me.

Once I saw Jessica's humanity, my perspective changed. I became aware, I couldn't just look past these girls anymore. I simply couldn't see them the same way. They were people, people whose lives had been interrupted by a horrible disease or circumstance. They were deserving of empathy and compassion. Maya Angelou once said, "We do what we do until we know better, once we know better, we do better." Jessica told me that, and, certainly, in that respect, Jessica made me better.

As the weeks grew closer to Jessica getting out, she had asked me if I could help her find a place to live. She had to have a physical address upon her release. At first, I was very reluctant, I knew how bad Jessica could get, knowing that it was a risk, but I was seeing a different side of her and starting to believe her. She would ask about coming to the gym and training with me; I told her absolutely and that she was certainly built for the part, which she was. I don't blow smoke up anybody's ass in that respect. She was very gifted genetically, long, lean frame, broad shoulders, wide back, long collar bones, great base, she had a booty and legs, she was built for my sport.

I started to imagine this person in my life, like REALLY in my life, above-board this time, somehow we could be some kind of new-age power couple, kicking ass! Training together, turning our lives around, getting her kids back, helping others. I created a whole imaginary scenario where we just moved on and created our own happily ever after. I talked to my ex-wife Lori. Now Lori and I were and still are the best of friends, so for me to introduce someone to her was a big thing. I knew she had a spare room and, after explaining the situation, if she would be willing to give Jess a shot. Lori is an optimist and trusted me and my judgment (god knows why), and we began to make some loose arrangements. I told Jessica, and she was ecstatic.

In all honesty, Jess and Lori would have really hit it off, now Jess might have tried to sleep with her, but you really can't hold that against her. Jess was supposed to call me the day before she got out, but I never heard from her. I went by Freddy's to check on her and make sure everything had gone as planned. As I drove up, I saw Jess in the front yard, and she was drunk, drunk as hell, fucked up already. I didn't get it; this wasn't part of the plan. After all, we had talked about all we shared, dreamed about, these great plans, the fucking "happily ever after"?? What the fuck!! There she was, right back where she started, and there I was a complete fool. I was immediately broken-hearted, utterly disillusioned. I got in my car and drove off.

She was yelling, "Tim!! Tim!! Baby!! It's no big deal!! Come back!!"

I never even looked in the rearview, just kept on driving.

Weeks had passed since I had seen or heard from Jess, so I got curious and took a drive down Charlotte. Sure enough, she was walking with some guy and broke off immediately when she saw my car.

I rolled down my window.

"How's tricks?" I popped off with a shit-eating grin.

"Fuck off!!"

She threw back without even blinking. Our snappy repartee had begun yet again. She asked if I was spying on her, and I told her I thought I was just checking on her and how she was doing.

"Yeah, well, that's spying."

Whatever, I mean, why should I have even given two fucks after she did what she did; I felt like I wanted to use the word betrayed there, I mean that's how it felt. After all, we had shared and planned, opened up to each other.....she didn't even give it a thought. Just threw it away. We continued for a bit, just digging up shit to say to hurt each other, things we knew. I have always thought it such a horrible breach to allow someone into your life, to share intimate details with them, and then when things start to go south, those details become projectiles, open game, weapons used against you.

With Jessica, this created an interesting duality because when Jess got pissed off, she wouldn't hold back. She would come at you with everything she had, anything she had learned about you, there were NO boundaries, except that, and herein lies the duality, that's not exactly true, there was one trust she never broke, and it still amazes me.

I shared an experience with her, an intensely personal one, a very ugly one. One I didn't talk about for a very long time and still don't discuss today. Why I shared it with her is just another one of those mysteries or further proof of the actual depths my stupidity can run...

Either way, when I lived in Tampa and was heavily into my addiction, I would pick up street girls to help me get dope. If we smoked it together, it was unlikely I would get ripped off. The thing about picking up on the street was that you never knew what you were going to get. This particular evening, I saw a girl walking and slowed down to pick her up when she got in, and I realized quickly this was a transsexual, not my thing, but when you're just trying to get some dope, it didn't really matter. Now not to be rude, but After she got in the car, it was fairly easy to see this was not a chick, and he explained that to me quickly as well, so as not to offend, I acted surprised. He asked if I was still interested, and I explained I didn't swing that way, boundaries set. He asked if I wanted to get high, and I was like, "damn skippy!"

We copped some hard and went to his apartment- I wouldn't call it a stretch to say it was a crack house. We sat there smoking with very light small talk when two of his friends came by. They also had some dope, so we all sat there getting high as fuck. As we sat, one made a sloppy pass at me; again, I kindly explained that I wasn't into guys, it just wasn't my thing, but he didn't accept the decline as graciously and kept it up, almost as if he was trying to convince me. He kept putting hands on me, and I kept deflecting his hands, suddenly his friend started too,, as well as my original company. Now we are talking Three on one.

Things went south quickly- I don't remember a lot from there. I remember short, vivid flashbacks, disgusting things I won't put in print, but the majority has been blocked out of my mind, even if I could remember, I wouldn't talk about it- suffice to say I was assaulted —the end.

Now, I shared THAT with Jessica. One night we were chatting, and she began talking about how many of the girls get assaulted and that she did her best to protect them, so I chimed in that it wasn't only women. She paused, and I very briefly shared that experience.

She looked at me, staring deeply into me, unlike any time before. She said, "that's why you all big like that, why you got all jacked...That's why you look the way you do, to protect yourself..."

I was exposed and scared. I regretted having said anything, but I was too far in. All I could do was to slowly nod my head. Again, she gave me a deep stare, as if to offer an unflinching resignation to what I just shared. Straight faced and allowing me a degree of dignity, she simply added, "that's what's up," and quickly changed the subject.

Just in some of the stories I've shared, one would think that the minute she got fired up, all that would come gushing out as an attack. I mean, that's a tough one for a guy.

She never mentioned it again. Not once. I cannot explain why, and to this day, I do not know.

Maybe she did have boundaries, the deep, dark kind. Personal experiences that once shared, need never be spoken of again.

When people read this and see all the craziness and insanity, they ask me how, why? Why the fuck would you stay and continue to deal with all of it?"

That's what I recall, that specific moment in time. I remember that loyalty, so deep, scarcely anyone on this planet could comprehend it, much less emulate it. Jessica was crazy, but she loved hard, was fiercely loyal, and once you were in her heart, she was, in the ways that really count, the truest friend.

MAYBE I'M THE ONE

So who is it? You start to wonder after reliving events over and over in your life, when you know the one common denominator is always you. Put this on and read

Maybe I'm the One
Puddle of Mudd

While she was in jail, Jess begged me time and time again to send her cards or to write her letters. I would tell her yes, nod my head like I was going to but never did; there was simply no way I was going to leave that kind of a footprint. I knew her better than that. Even if I was green, I wasn't stupid. Turns out, I was right in my restraint. Apparently, one of her peeps had been sending her all kinds of love letters.

Guess he didn't get the memo. Keep in mind, if it wasn't for this jackass and his stupidity in allowing Jess to drive, she wouldn't even have been in jail.

So, a married man with shit to lose, sending love letters to his trick in jail, that's some next-level stupid right there. Of course, Jess saved every letter, every card, each one signed by the man himself.

Blackmail is a hell of a thing.

I drove up on her at Freddy's, where she was outside having a heated conversation.

"Well then motherfucker, guess I'll just have to show your wife all these fucking letters your dumbass sent me, won't I?"

UH-OH! Somebody fucked up!!

Yup, straight up blackmail- or was it extortion? I'm really not sure, but either way, she was getting money from, and I agree with her here, his dumb ass. Why the fuck you would give Jess any potential ammo is beyond me. Jessica was always incredibly resourceful, any edge, any angle she could exploit, and you could guarantee she would be on it. If it wasn't organic, she would manufacture it. Her mind moved quickly. Generally, it revolved around figuring out how to score dope, either directly or to get money to buy dope.

She once shared with me that her stint in prison gave her the skillset to become a more effective 'criminal.' I think, in truth, it merely made her a more efficient addict. The "criminal" label was collateral damage. I don't believe she saw then what I see now, namely that addicts and/or the mentally ill who enter "the system" do not receive any treatment whatsoever, because they aren't identified as such, as addicts, as sick. There is very little consideration for their well-being or betterment. If they weren't criminals upon entering, they quickly become acclimated to that element.

Jess and I walked into an Asian market one day, I purchased a box of ginseng shooters. When I opened the box to get one of the shooters, she noticed the bottle.

I could see the wheels start turning. She looked at the box and asked, "That's what's in there? How much did that whole box cost?"

"Yeah, Ginseng shots, it's like nine bucks."

"How many are in it?"

"Twelve."

She got on the phone immediately,

"Check this out, I can make twelve stems for just under $10. We sell them for $5 each, right? K, I'm on it."

She hung up and turned to me.

"Can you buy me one of those?"

Huh? I had no idea where this was going.

I said, "sure, what's the deal though, you have a friend that likes these?"

"I can make crack stems out of those and sell them for $5 each, so I can make $50 0ff of $10."

Wow.

She was amazing in many ways, some good, some bad, some neither, just a means to an end.

The everyday, "matter of fact" way she was handling, it was something to be marveled.

Some things were spur of the moment, pure happenstance. She would jump onsite with both feet. Other things were a slow roll, set up weeks in advance like some dope acquiring sting operation.

She had made mention that she was eating like a horse and gaining weight. I didn't pay it any mind, until one day she stopped and said, "I know you can see I'm getting a belly, but you haven't even asked."

I did not see this "belly" of which she spoke, but now...

The game was afoot.

"I'm pregnant."

Jess was pregnant.

By- me.

Ok.

Of course, it seemed she had forgotten or just didn't care (because it didn't fit in with her narrative) that she had already shared with me that she had her tubes tied after her last pregnancy. Ergo, there should have been no way she could have gotten pregnant, well, there was no way, but that did not matter. Somehow, someway, I had gotten Jess pregnant.

I told her repeatedly that I didn't believe her. When I offered to buy her a pregnancy test, she declined. There was no proof whatsoever that she was genuinely pregnant, but because she said she was, that's the way it was. She did bring me a pregnancy test strip that showed a positive. Still, when I requested, again, that I get her one so we could do it together, she also declined the invitation.

Look, I knew she was not pregnant. She had already told me she couldn't get pregnant. This was a play, but let's be real- that didn't matter, not to her, nor did it matter to her "friends." She built it up so much that it developed a life of its own. She told everyone she could that "we" were having a baby. This opened up a world of opportunity for her.

She portrayed me as the bad guy who got her pregnant, refused to help, and denied everything. She played the pity card every chance she could. Mostly for places to stay, food, money. This was one of those well-laid plans, a "sting" if you will. While I admit it was well played, I did begin to wonder how on earth this charade was going to play out. I mean- it was already curious to me how she was able to keep up the masquerade with others. Especially while she was still using daily.

But somehow, she did.

As the whole show rolled on, her time began to run out. There is a time limit on this particular type of con. Seven to Nine months being the end game. If you aren't seriously bellied up by 7-8 months, people are going to start asking questions.

Her solution?

Jess decided she was going to abort the baby. She never asked for my input. We never discussed it. She didn't ask for a penny, which was telling. What Jess did do was set up a trip to Ohio. She had an ex-girlfriend up there and claimed she had a doctor friend who would "take care" of it. So, the next step was transportation. I remained steadfast that this was just another one of her plays.

She told everyone and their brother what a piece of shit I was and refused to help in any way. This wasn't exactly true. After her "friend" got her a bus ticket, I did drive her to the bus station. I sat with her as she ate Xanax after Xanax, and, finally, just before she left, I gave her some cash for food and made sure she made the right bus. She was nervous to be certain; she had never been on a bus and only had the $30-

40 bucks I had given her. She wasn't convinced until they gave the last call for the bus. She sloppily kissed me before staggering her benzo'd ass onto the bus, calling me every ten minutes until she passed out.

The next day I got the call. She had made it safe and sound to Ohio. Her girlfriend picked her up, and the drinking and debauchery had begun. For me, the trip was a blur, random texts, random calls, fights, and then, toward the end, it seemed I learned the actual name of that "old friend" she had spoken of so often, heroin.

She would call, low, quiet voice, slurred speech, pauses that lasted 10+ minutes. She would nod in and out of consciousness. I would stay on the phone the whole time and suffer through her visit to her "old friend."

Like so many things between Jess and me, it was scary at first. Well, If I'm being 1000, it wasn't exactly the first time I had seen her and her old friend. I found her passed out face first in the front yard at Mr. Davis's one day with a rig in her hand. When she came to, she fessed up as to what was going on. I thought it was merely an isolated incident, which in Tallahassee, it was. Not so much where she went. Either way, scary, very scary.

She would wake up incoherent, asking who she was talking to, or nod off snoring into her phone. Indeed, she had missed that old friend and was making up for lost time. She dropped off for an hour or so at one point. I was concerned but quite literally had no way to get in touch or contact anyone for help. Her phone died, and I was panicked. She had mentioned a train station, but where? Somewhere in Ohio was all I knew.

Finally, I got a call. A couple of people had found her passed out in the train station. She was completely out, so they called 911. Somebody had taken the time to charge her phone and called the last number on there, me.

As we were speaking, getting her information, what had she been doing? History of drug issues? I answered as best I could. As they worked, I never heard a peep out of Jess. Suddenly, they gave her something, and she was UP! Yelling, screaming at the EMT's. She got on the phone with me, and I attempted to calm her down. She didn't remember much, so I helped her piece together how she got there. She was a mess. She broke down, crying, the long wailing cries, the ugly cry. She was done; she didn't want to be there anymore. She just wanted to come "home."

"Please just let me come back. Please, please, please! I don't want to be here! I don't belong here anymore."

Her pleas were wailing and long. She hardly had time to catch her breath between sobs. Her voice would crack, and my heart was shattered for her. It was so hard to listen. I took over,

"Jess, You Get me what I need to get you a bus ticket back. You can come back, nothings stopping you, nothing ever was."

There he was, The Caretaker, Mr. Fixer-upper. My therapist once told me that I had a thing for "fixer-uppers" in relationships, A tendency to gravitate toward the broken, the baby birds who cannot fly. I tried to pick them up and help them fly again. Sounded good at first glance, all noble and shit, but don't get the idea that this was some saintly quality.

It wasn't.

It's not an altruistic feature: It makes ME feel better about myself. It is, by definition, self-serving.

Many of an addict's actions, using or not, are still based on the self-centered nature of the disease.

Helping her gave me something that I needed just as much as it may have "helped" her.

If you "help" a baby bird in the real world, it is often not accepted back into the nest. It is rejected. It can be a death sentence.

I knew none of that then, nor would I have cared had I known. Jess got me all the info I needed, and I got her a ticket back "home" no stalling, no hesitation. It seemed her "old friend" had taken her face to face with the abyss yet again, but this time she bolted, ran the fuck away, not backing out or stepping to the side, RUNNING the fuck away! In some way, her immediate recoil, how she jumped back, away from the heat, made me proud of her. Growth. It is a painful process, but the pain of staying where you are, especially as an addict, has far dire consequences.

She must have slept for most of the bus ride because we didn't talk much. When I picked her up from the bus station, the ride was quiet. She hardly spoke, and I didn't know what to say. I put her up in a hotel for a couple nights, she slept for two days straight. She only woke up to eat. She did tell me that everything went well with her "procedure" still no proof, no papers, no instructions, nothing.

I didn't care. I was glad she was back; she was safe. And yes, I missed her. She was the coolest person I knew. She quickly found a place to "recover" from the procedure, a girlfriend's place. I, of course, was still the bad guy. Even worse now, I forced her to have an abortion. I dropped her at the bus station, gave her $20, and sent her off to handle it. It was great material for her to get the sympathy she needed.

Again, me being the total bad guy, like something out of a movie. Her street girlfriends all hated me. She would call, and I would hear them making comments in the background.

"Piece of shit."

"Gonna get what you deserve."

Jess played the part well. She would defend me half-heartedly on the phone - then hang up and tell them all how controlling I was, wouldn't let her talk to people, jacked up on steroids, violent.

I certainly looked the part... So it wasn't hard for the inexperienced girls to believe Jessica's sad stories. But the girls who knew Jess- really knew Jess- also understood just how ridiculous this all was. Jess wasn't controlled by anyone, not even herself. To know Jessica was to realize that all these things she was saying were lies designed to help her manipulate the situation to her benefit.

The strangest part to me was that when we were together, one on one, she and I were fine. Ok, well, as fine as two fucked up people can be. But my point is that the shit she was telling them never entered into our own interpersonal relationship; there was a disconnect. Such a disconnect that it was almost like two different people. Jess with me versus Jess in front of other people.

She was getting more possessive of me, of our time together, while cementing her picture of my other side, "Mr. Hyde," if you will. Meanwhile, her trip had done nothing for her addiction. Her drinking was out of control. I was getting calls daily to come to get her, either for fighting or passing out somewhere. One day I finally asked her how on earth she thought we could have any semblance of a relationship while she was using so heavily.

"You gonna check me into rehab? You want to watch that again?"

I didn't have that kind of money, but instead, I asked, "Have you ever tried it on your own? I mean, what do you need? They didn't do shit for you in jail, and you came through it."

Suddenly, boom- "Do you want me in your life, Tim?"

Whew! That was way too much for me at that point, but I waded in a little, "What if I did? I mean, as far as you and I go, we really do not know anything. You stay fucked almost every day. I'm thinking, more than likely, once you got clean, you would probably never want to see me again."

I was laughing it off, but THAT QUESTION.

Do you want me in your life?

It made me think. Then when she shot back.

"I am willing to try."

It made me think more. Now she was staring at me, studying my face, my reaction.

Oh shit, now what? I stammered into a, "Well, you know I can't afford rehab. How would we even start?"

"Let me stay with you for a week, you'll just have to keep a little liquor on hand to help me when the shakes start."

I could not do it that way.

My son. My son and I lived together. No way I was going to put him through that. So I suggested a hotel—a few days in a hotel where we could help her detox.

I paid for four days upfront. I took her phone. I kept some simple foods in the room, white bread, saltines, Gatorade but carried the alcohol with me. I still had to work, so I would check on her every couple of hours. It got bad quickly.

She was violently shaking, sweating, puking. The smell of the room was something that one could never forget.

She fought tooth and nail. Her determination was rock solid, admirable even.

I was scared- terrified. People die from this shit! This wasn't a joke; it wasn't a DIY project. A thousand things could go wrong. My deepest fear was that I would leave for work, and by the time I got back, Jess would have died, asphyxiation, shock, whatever the fuck else could kill you from DTS!!

Arrogant... That was me, to think I/we could pull this off, reckless and arrogant. I liked to think of it as a kind of self-confidence, a belief in myself, and my ability to handle shit, but that was a rationalization. It was straight-up unflinching arrogance. After the second day, I told her I thought she should go to detox. My timing could not have been worse. She begged me not to take her, swore she was on the other side of it. She asked me to trust her, to believe in her.

I didn't see it then, but Jess was trying to prove something to me and not just the fact that she was able to detox on her own, she was showing me what she was willing to go through for there to even be a chance at an "us." I just missed it. Plain as day, right in front of me, but blind to what she was really trying to say.

I took her to the detox. She was too weak, too exhausted to even fight me. She cried, sobbing yet again. She didn't want to be there. This wasn't part of her plan. She wanted to do this with me for us. I had panicked; If you haven't seen what a detox looks like, you have no idea how frightening it is, how bad it gets. She told me she could do this, but I didn't trust her judgment enough, not in that moment, it was skewed. That was par for the course for us, Just constantly out of sync, that was our MO.

Our only synchronicity was in the inevitability we shared in taking turns breaking each other's hearts.

She stayed in detox for 3 days. I came and visited her, but it was very impersonal. No hugging, no touching. Could only visit 15 minutes. She was very down. This was not what she wanted, at a minimum, not the way she wanted. I got that, I knew she was upset, but I also knew she would survive.

It was far safer.

When Jess got out, she went straight back to it. Without hesitation. Of course, she told me it was all my fault, I didn't let her do it on her own. I "ruined it" I don't know... maybe I had, but this wasn't the end. We still limped forward.

While Jessica and I had more than enough challenges between us, any one of which could have stopped us dead in our tracks. I always go back to a conversation I had with a friend many years before regarding relationships.

He told me that there are only really two basic things that you need for a relationship.

Only two, but each is essential: *Chemistry and Timing.*

Chemistry is that physical attraction you feel on almost a primal level- its either there or it is not. There's no faking it.

And timing?

Well, that timing...

It's a bitch.

BAD GIRLFRIEND

Because everybody wants that badass in their life. Though many times, in wanting it so badly, concessions are made. The lines in the sand are gone, but our ego is fed. Just listen to this one.

Bad Girlfriend

Theory of a Deadman

At this point, Jessica was all in. She had decided that she wanted the whole Pretty Woman scenario and set her mind to, somehow, making this all work out. She regularly started telling me, "Oh, I'm gonna have my happy ending, I know it. I love you more than I have ever loved anybody, you watch."

On a drive one day, out of the blue, she turned to me and said, "You know you're my lobster, right?"

I didn't get the reference.

She was looking at me under her hat with her cutest little sideways glance. She explained, "My lobster! See, lobsters' mate for life, no matter what! If they become separated, for whatever reason, storms, earth-quakes, anything, they always find their way back to each other. Once they mate, that's it; its forever. That's you and me. I just gotta get right so we can have our happy ending."

There she was.

Yet again, capturing my heart with this incredibly romantic notion.

I was flattered- like truly and honestly flattered. I wanted it, too. Jessica was gorgeous, strong, dangerous, and, at her best, Loving and romantic. The way I saw it, on top of those qualites, here was this hot, badass street girl, this smokin' hood rat wanting me, ME? She could have anybody (no jokes, please) but somehow, this fucked up white boy had won her affection? The upside was win/win. My ego is no small thing.

Now I knew that much of Jessica's newfound interest in "us" was her playing her games, manipulation. So I kept my guard up, but I was falling for her straight up. I would not admit it, but it was apparently evident to many who knew me. Much to their chagrin, I might add. I knew who she was, where she was in that moment, but I also believed, I knew, there was so much more, her potential, who and what she could be. My friends thought I was crazy.

Too often, we see angels in the demons in our lives. Keep in mind the devil was once an angel.

As I walked into work one day, still dealing with Jessica on the phone, one of my cooks, Charles - who had heard all of the drama and craziness with Jess over the years and especially over the recent months - was listening to me ramble on about "crazy" Jessica. After I had hung up, he stopped me and said, "You know you love her, right?"

I stopped, "What?"

He repeated it, "You know you love her, that's your fuckin' Boo, the heart wants what the heart wants, it's OK."

I immediately backtracked. "I don't love her; she's fucking crazy. I mean we have fun, we've always had fun, but that's all there is to it, there's no future there, there can't be-"

He finished with, "OK, OK, I hear what you're saying, but I also know, like it or not, that IS your Boo, you can't help it!" With a shrug of his shoulders, he threw in, "the heart wants what the heart wants..."

That little exchange exposed me. I knew he was right, as much as I hated to admit it, he was right.

I remember an exchange we had. As she was getting out of the car, Jess said, "I love you, baby."

In my asshole-ish non-committal way, I responded, "Oh, I believe you do." But this time she was not taking that bullshit answer, "Do you love me, Tim?"

After all, I've shared, the craziness and such, You might think otherwise, but it was easy to say,

"Yes, Jess, I love you, you have to know I love you by now, I wouldn't be here otherwise."

I had taken the bait, without hesitation, she snapped, "You should really say that more often, it sounds good."

A sly little smile and all......

She'd been staying with a guy she had been dealing to, named Thomas, having worn out yet another welcome elsewhere. Now, Thomas, I liked. He was a big friendly guy and always invited me in, and we would chat about whatever he was good people. The fact that he was gay did not hurt my feelings, either. More than that, though, Thomas understood how Jessica felt about me. He would share with me the things I was not around to hear. It meant a lot to me to start to understand who she was when I wasn't looking, and he gave me great insight. I was also reasonably sure Jess was fucking his other female roommate, but what else was new?

Thomas called me, terribly upset, Jess had lost it, yet again. He had seen her spewing venom at me but hadn't yet had it turned on him. By his account, something had gone wrong; drug deal, money, who knows but she was triggered. Each of them had different stories. When you're dealing with drugs and addictions, the truth all depends on which side of the deal you're on. Some crack came up missing, so Jess, of course, believed Thomas had stolen it, and,

CLICK.

She was outside, screaming at the top of her lungs about Thomas.

Thomas helped several neighborhood families by watching their kids. He was also HIV positive, very open about it with friends but understandably guarded with the outside world. Well, Jessica was screaming to everyone in earshot that he was HIV positive and that they shouldn't leave their kids with him, rambling on, making a huge scene. Thomas was so hurt, completely betrayed, he called me to come to get her. She wasn't welcome anymore. I felt horrible for him, apologizing for Jessica. I came and got her, just to spare him the embarrassment. I picked her up and asked her what the fuck had happened.

The Jess story was he stole a bunch of crack and had no way to pay for it, and she lost it, No remorse, it was his fault. I don't really know why I bothered asking. I knew what her answer would be. Jessica wasn't about to take any responsibility; she didn't apologize, it just wasn't in her. With all she had been through, I believe she simply couldn't take any more ownership, she couldn't accept anything else on her conscience, then again, maybe I'm still making excuses for her.

She brought a basket of clothes with her. My son wasn't there that day, so, like a fool, I agreed to let her stay till she could make other arrangements. As the evening wore on, Jess started up, wanting some liquor, needed a ride to get "something" I wasn't about to go that direction, so it started getting loud. I finally asked her to leave, just take her shit and go. Nope, there she sat, on the floor, refusing to leave, going through her things, and steadily cursing me. Since the beginning, Jess had called me everything but a Christian. I told her I was going to call the law to have her removed.

She looked up at me very matter-of-factly and said, "Really?" nodding her head at me. "Here, watch this."

She reached her hand to her throat and scratched across it, leaving four deep blood trails.

She immediately dialed 911 and said, "My boyfriend just tried to strangle me, I need help." It was a calm, cool-headed voice, smiling at me the entire time she spoke.

I was stunned, was this really happening?? Is she really doing this?? I was dumbfounded, I immediately called 911 as well, "What is your emergency?"

"I have a girl in my house who is threatening me and refusing to leave."

The dispatcher asked if I was safe, and I told her I felt I was OK. She also told me this was county jurisdiction, and she would transfer me to the county, but first, she asked if the woman of whom I was speaking had called 911 first.

I told the dispatcher Jess was on the phone with them now,

to which the dispatcher replied, "Uh yeah, she is talking to the city right now." The womanthen transferred me to the county operator, and I explained the situation.

Jess was off the phone now and started talking to me, "Tim, just hang up the phone, let's work this out, come on, it's me, let's talk."

It was always scary how quickly she could flip the switch from trying to force your hand to suddenly being reasonable. I gave the operator her name, and she paused, "Sir, do you know this woman?"

I told her I had been associated with her for a while now, but that tonight she was just out of control and needed to go. The 911 operator was very serious, "Sir, I have her record up on my screen. She has a history of violence. I suggest you lock yourself in a room until we arrive."

Lock myself in my room?? Oh, Hell, no!! I was not leaving her alone in my frigging house!

Meanwhile, Jess was up in my face, calm, reasoning, measured. "You better hang up, Tim, this isn't going to go well for you, I'm telling you some good shit right now, hang up now. We can leave and talk this out, you're fucking up, you already know who they're going to believe."

I stayed on the phone while she was talking to me, back against the wall. Suddenly Jessica leaned in very close to my ear and whispered slowly and clearly in a breathy lilt, "You're gonna go to jail."

She was staring me right in the eyes as she breathed it out; it was chilling. Jess very slowly drifted back away, still staring me in the eyes, a half-smile on her face. As she moved away, she said she was stepping out back to smoke a cigarette before they got there, "I wanna be ready for this show."

I sat and waited, scared as hell, was That true?? Would they believe that story? Finally, a knock on the door. I opened it up, and a deputy came in. He immediately asked where she was. I said she had gone out back to smoke. When he went to check, Jess was gone. She had jumped the fence and ran. The deputy mulled around my living room, doing cop shit, faking small talk so he could scan for any contraband. He warned me not to let her come back, to file a trespass warrant to protect myself, but, as usual, I declined. He looked over my coffee table one more time and left. I locked the door and went to bed, wore out. It was an emotional tired, a tired I had grown quite accustomed too.

Despite her little detour, Jessica was trying hard to hold it together, something I desperately wanted as well. She moved about a half-hour out of town with a former client named Steve. I knew Jess had been fucking him, that's how they met, but she, of course, denied having ever even seen him without his hat. At this point, despite her track record, I believed it was not a sexual relationship, Steve was intimidated by me and made it a point to reiterate it time and time again, and even Thomas threw me a bone on that one, saying he believed it to be plutonic. Jess was legitimately trying.

So out in the country, she went. No air conditioning, good ole Florida windows, and lots of ceiling fans. The house all wood in the middle of a huge field. It was actually very quaint. BY Jessica's own volition, she wouldn't be drinking or drugging while she was out there. I made the drive almost daily; I'd call while I was driving there, and she'd be naked upstairs when I arrived. Again, at this point for both of us, we were more like boyfriend and girlfriend, so no money was exchanged, but I would take her out to dinner, we would eat, listen to whatever music was playing, and cut up together. Those were some of the best moments with her. She would ramble about her crazy life, concerts, fights, anything that came to her mind. I'd share some of my exploits from the road, stage, or kitchen. We'd dance in our seats when some good tunes came on. She'd make fun of my white boy moves.

"What the fuck is up with that stiff-arm shit??"

Whatever.

She had no room to talk. She had moves, like Elaine on Seinfeld, well, unless she did the stripper thing, she had few decent stripper moves, but that was it). We would finish up, and I'd ask what she was doing for the rest of the night, invariably "You, if you'd let me," a standard Jessica response, to anyone, unfortunately, but she was always cute in saying it, as in so many things. Jessica could be utterly amazing anytime she chose to be. It was all those facets, this amalgam, of good and bad, ugly and beautiful, it was her duality I loved. In being a little bit of everything, she was unapologetic.

"Baby, I know I'm a mess, but think about this, all things considered, if the shit all came down one night and you had to make one call: Who would you call? Who would you want to have your back 1000?!?"

Certain moments, good or bad, just stick with you.

Valentine's Day. Jess was still struggling. Treading water at best. I knew it wouldn't be long before something big and potentially bad happened. As was my custom, I wanted to help, Mr. Fixer, remember? Some might call it codependent. They would be right. As I said, little I did was completely altruistic, so, again, it was as much about helping my ego, my self-esteem, as it ever was about helping her.

That being said, I developed "the plan."

I had just the thing! A dog! A puppy, no less!! something to force her outside herself, to care about something other than just getting high.

That was my thought anyway.

I found a puppy, a chihuahua mix (it was NOT, but that is what I was told). I dressed her up with a bow, put her in a box with heart wrapping paper, a rose on top. I can't lie. My ego was over the top, Captain Save-a-Hoe, this simple act would be the catalyst to completely turning her around. I will be revered as a fucking hero!! Look at how cool I am!! in case you haven't figured it out by now, I'm an idiot.

So, I show up, puppy in tow, all excited. I went to knock on the door but found it partially open. I said her name, "Jess?" I slowly opened the door, there is Jess passed out on the couch, drooling, needle still in her arm. I stood there in shock, completely lost. I immediately checked her pulse, slow but fine. Breathing was good. She nodded in and out. Occasionally, she would try to say something but couldn't get anything intelligible out. I got the rig out of her arm. She was still in and out but more responsive, on the upside of it. I stood back up, still surveying the scene when it hit me all at once.

What the fuck was I thinking? Was I that far gone?? Giving her charge of another living creature? She had already lost her kids, did that not send up a red flag or two? It is amazing how quickly one can go from a super fucking hero to the penitent buffoon. She nodded off again, I left. Never took the dog out, no card, no roses, nothing.

When you set yourself up to be disappointed, who do you have to blame?

So now I had a dog, a puppy no less. I took her home. Feeling the fool would be an understatement. Let's see, food and water bowls, leash, all the accompanying accouterments. Didn't take long for Jess to call.

The lies to make oneself look better, especially after such a debacle, those are the good ones -I like the pretty lies. She started with: she was just very tired, had been up all night, no sleep.

Uh, huh, and you had a big shot of heroin!! That'll make you tired.

I said, "Happy Valentines Day."

She, of course, came back with, "Where's my present?"

Uh Yeah.

"Baby, you missed out on your present, she was all ready to see you, wrapped with a bow and all, but you were passed out on the couch, with a fucking needle in your arm so I couldn't bring myself to leave her."

Puzzled, she asked, "Her, who?"

Now she had taken the bait, "Well, I had got you a dog, a puppy."

No response, not a peep, the wheels were spinning. On the one hand, she was trying to figure out what I knew and what I didn't know, but also if I was just fucking with her about the dog.

She laughed it off,

"You fucking liar, you didn't get a dog, you're not that stupid."

"Actually, I am that stupid, well, I was that stupid, I've decided I'm going to keep her now; she'll be better off with me."

She continued on, "There's no fucking way you got me a dog. What kind of dog, then? What does she look like?"

We went back and forth, playing twenty questions. I sent pics, she denied every one. I couldn't tell if she legitimately didn't believe me or if she was just trying to figure an angle to get her present anyway.

A few days had passed, and Bren, short for Brenoise (a French culinary term referring to a small dice), was getting comfortable. I decided to bring Jess over to see her.

She just stared at her at first.

"I thought you said she was a chihuahua?"

I told her she was part chihuahua, she laughed, "Which part?? there ain't much chihuahua in that fucking mutt!"

Despite her sour grapes attitude, she warmed up to her quickly, then I got every bit of advice she knew,

"You need to carry her, they like to be carried. Make sure you make her feel secure, they hate not having consistency..."

Food, water, how to walk, Jess became an authority on half breed chihuahuas, and I loved it. While I still didn't think she should own the pup, she was already starting to care for her, at least sounding responsible. I mean, I was willing to take what I could get, any improvement, anything that might break her regular routine or MO. I was trying.

I wanted Jess in my life, but, again, if I'm keeping it real, like really, real, maybe even 1000: most times I didn't help.

Not giving her the pup might have been the right decision but the need to tell her I that I wasn't? She didn't even know about the puppy, so why tell her? That was punishment, that was vindictive. That was not what Jess needed; consequences had no effect on her. That was just me being an ass, hurt, and wanting to hurt her back, unproductive. As I look back, I realize that she told me a lot, I just didn't listen, too self-absorbed, just unwilling. She told me though, "'OK, I have to stay at this guy's place tonight, I don't have anywhere else to go..." the pauses, those little nuances, she was saying, "I am in survival mode, I need shelter, I need food, if you don't help me, I will stay with whomever, and in whatever form that takes..."

I'm not saying I would have just stopped everything and helped. The thing is, I didn't even listen, couldn't hear what she was saying or choosing not to.

I learned a word that I have grown to embrace - *Einfühlung*, it doesn't translate exactly, but the concept is universal: to empathy, to feel into, perhaps more along the line of a means to evoke an emotion.

She told me these things often, about money, about places to stay, needing food, hints to clue me in, to feel what it was like in her world, but I would not allow myself to get to those feelings. Maybe it was just too overwhelming for me as the "empath" I like to fancy myself or worse: I just chose not to care. You handle your business, so long as I got what I wanted, everything was good in the hood. One of the hardest parts for me, in retrospect, is coming to realize that someone you claimed to love, someone you knew was struggling, was actually **telling** you all along that they were drowning, telling you what they would have to do to survive the night, even asking for help between the lines, and you simply let them flounder and go under time and time again.

No one really treads water. You're either fighting against the current or going back downstream.

WICKED GAME

When it all starts to unravel, that's when you discover the cost of allowing someone in, especially the pretty ones. Listen while you read

Wicked Game

Chris Isaak

I knew Jess had been just holding on, so the call from Steve wasn't a huge surprise. He started with an apology, never a good sign. He was sorry for lying to me about the way he and Jess had met. An interesting gesture as it sounded more like he was "tattling" on Jess, and, let's be real, it wasn't like I didn't know already. Still, he apparently felt the need to unload the weight of his deception. I dismissed it with an insincere 'thank you' so that he could start on the real reason he called.

Jess had lost it.

By his account, her restlessness had reached its precipice late that night. She asked him for a ride into town when Steve declined, she became insistent. A shouting match ensued, things escalated; and, as per her script, police ended up getting involved. It took a bad turn for Steve in this case as he was asked to leave, Jess had no money, and no way to leave or any means to support herself. Whereas Steve was gainfully employed and had a vehicle. No brainer for the cops; once he is gone, the situation is defused. Steve complied, returning the next day only to find that Jess was nowhere to be found, but, true to form, she had destroyed his place. Broke all the windows, broke his TV, slashed the screens, smashed glasses and plates. Suffice it to say, if you could break it, it was broken.

Now, this was nothing new. Anyone who had been around Jess for any time knew that she could click at any time. As such, they knew she was capable of just about anything once that happened. Yet, it was always a surprise, and, inevitably, in those days, I would get a call. Why? I don't know, maybe because there was really nothing else you could do, but, in most cases, after seeing the wrath Jess could bring down, they were scared to death of her. They would call me to see if I could be an intermediary, for what exactly? Again, I have no idea, but for whatever reason, they called.

It never worked out for them because of several dynamics. First off, in my mind: You play, you pay. They knew what could happen, they played, they lost, charge that shit to the game. Secondly, I had little to no influence over Jess.

She was a free radical in all senses of the word- asking me to rein her in was like asking me to teach a cat to speak French: A complete waste of my time and a great way to annoy the cat.

Steve's main concern was for his job. Jess made threats regarding his work, and he was apprehensive about just how far she would go. He asked if she had ever made threats like this toward me and, if so, had she followed through with any of them. What could I say? She made threats all the time, most never followed up on, but she wasn't exactly consistent in her reactions. I tried to calm him down as best I could before I turned my attention to Jess. I knew WHAT she was doing, for the most part, but where and with whom, not so much. Her phone had been disconnected or shut off. All I could really do was to sit and wait for her to resurface.

Eventually, I got the call. Jess was at the hospital, an ER tech called me to come and give her a ride so she could be discharged. When I got there, she was quiet, the ER Doctor was talking with her, she had a handful of paperwork. I didn't say a word, I knew it was coming, but I wasn't about to push. She said she was sorry and asked if I had spoken with Steve.

I said, of course, she stopped me quick, "Don't believe what that motherfucker says, there's a lot more to it than what he told you."

I asked her how she could know what He had told me.

"Because he told me exactly what he was gonna say. We got in a fight, and motherfucker started threatening me about telling you some fucked up shit about me to break us up. I told him some good shit. But he was all up on that fuck shit, so motherfucker paid the price, got what he deserved!"

As usual, never her fault, but then to be real, how often does anyone do some fucked up shit and just own up to it.

Cop: "do you have any drugs in the car?"

Driver: "Sure!! Tons of them!!"

Doesn't happen.

Same story: 3 sides, 3 dynamics.

Now Jessica's response was undoubtedly over the top. I knew there was so much more to it, but digging into it, especially right then, was just a waste of time. She didn't need it, I didn't need it, and guaranteed to start a fight.

My thought on that sort of escalation is this. Never, ever, have two people escalated a discussion to screaming at each other, each one trying to prove their point when one of them suddenly stops and says, "Oh my God! You're right!! I am such an idiot, I should have seen that all along!!" It just doesn't happen, let it go, pick your battles.

The ride remained quiet, uncomfortably quiet. Jess seemed lost in thought, so I finally asked how she ended up at the ER. She said she didn't know, she just woke up there. The paramedics told her she was found unconscious in someone's front yard, half-dressed. The people who lived there found her and called 911. She had an idea where she was or how she got there. She was taken to the ER to be checked out. A blood test showed she had Rohypnol in her system, among other things; Rohypnol–the date rape drug. I sat, trying to process what she was saying. I glanced at the mound of paperwork and noticed some medication as well. I asked what they had given her, nonchalantly she told me that it was the "Morning-after pill."

Wha??

"I didn't tell them I had my tubes tied, that's just procedure."

"What the fuck are you saying, Jess?"

"Look, It's no big deal, I may have been raped, I don't know, I can't remember anything after the Gas station."

No big deal??

"What the Fuck!! So how the fuck is that no big deal?!?"

She shot back, "It's not like it's the first time. This is what happens out here! This is my life! You just don't want to hear it! If you really loved me, if you really cared, you would listen, you'd hear me when I tell this shit! You should let me stay with you."

Ouch.

It wasn't like that thought hadn't crossed my mind many times. But her unpredictability, her downright dangerous nature always held me back. I had a son, a home, a business, I had shit to lose. Would it have helped? Her living with me? I don't know. I just don't know. Simply put, to this day, I don't know what the answer was, I don't know if there even was an answer, let alone a right answer, a "right" way to do things. Years later, I still have no answers.

It seems often, the puzzles, the questions life poses us, are of the rhetorical type.

I didn't respond, I couldn't, I didn't know what to say.

We sat there for a minute with a thickness in the air, now even more uncomfortable. She nodded and went with, "alright, then."

She asked me to take her to a friend's house. That she had found a place to stay.

By her story, this friend was one that her mom knew and that she had made arrangements for her to stay and recover for a few weeks.

Enter Mr. Cole.

Mr. Cole was a physically challenged older gentleman who apparently had taken a shine to, and subsequently offered Jess a place to stay. I took Jess to his house, and uncomfortable introductions were made. Jess directed most of the initial conversation, keeping the two of us from engaging. But when she left to go to the bathroom, I asked how he knew Jessica's mother. He looked at me sideways, almost surprised, and said,

"Her mother? I didn't even know Jessica until last night."

He further explained that he had called a friend to have a girl sent over. When Jess showed up, she convinced him to take her to buy some hard (crack), which he did. Still, when they got back to his place, he related that she was just too jacked up and wanting to get high to pay him any attention. They didn't do anything, she made a call, and she left.

I'm sorry?? What the fuck?!? This was a new wrinkle. She had a pimp or, at a minimum, worked for an escort service?

He told me the next time he heard from Jess was when she called him from the hospital that morning. She loosely explained what had happened after she left him. Further, she asked if she could rent his spare bedroom, including that she had a boyfriend who was "all jacked up on steroids and out of control jealous." She also clarified that he really didn't need to know about the way they had met.

He continued, "I was worried when I saw you, but I could tell right when we talked that wasn't you. If I would've known she had a boyfriend, I never would have let her come over".

On top of what had already happened, I could feel the emotion building. Still stunned and trying to take this newest wrinkle in, I said, "Who did you call? How did they know her?"

Before he could answer, Jess was back, with a nervous laugh, she shot out, "You motherfucker's better not have been talking about me?"

With my usual shit-eating grin, I said, "Well, not you, exactly, I was just wondering who your fucking pimp is, and why haven't I met him?"

She had nothing.

Her jaw dropped; I could see the wheels spinning in her head.

"Tim, it's not like that, the guy who gave me a ride asked me to come and keep Mr. Cole company and help take care of him."

If nothing else, Jess could lie her ass off with the quickness when she needed too, but this time there was another dynamic she couldn't control.

I turned to Mr. Cole and asked, "Is that how all this went down?"

He immediately backtracked, "Don't fucking put me in the middle of this. That's all on you, you two need to handle your business, leave me out of it."

She jumped on that one, "Yeah, baby, let's go, we'll get something to eat, and we'll talk, I'll tell you anything you want to know, he doesn't need to be all up in our business."

Now I was becoming the guy she always painted me to be. The emotion, the anger still building, all I could think was, this motherfucker had just come clean on what went down, and now he was looking for a way out.

"You were talking all kinds of shit just a minute ago, and now it's just between her and me. How bout, fuck you, Mr. Cole!!"

I spat his name with the same tone Jess spat Missy Lynn.

"You can get the fuck out of my house now, like, right now, before I call the law."

"Call the law?? Really!? And tell them what? You had a hooker come over and bought her crack, you piece of shit? Again, fuck you!!"

I started to get really angry, hands were shaking, face flushing, and I could see he was getting very nervous.

Jess tried to defuse it, "Come on, Tim. It's my fault, let's go talk, I'll explain everything."

He followed it up. "You best do what she says before you make some bad decisions, son."

"Bad decisions?? Motherfucker, that's the name of my fucking biography."

I knew I said it, but it sounded like Jess, that wasn't good. On top of that, quite frankly...

He was right, and I hated it. I wanted so bad to lose it. I had every reason, but I also have a deep fear of small spaces and orange. I needed to leave before this escalated into some Natural Born Killers scenario. I was staring Mr. Cole dead in the eye, gritting my teeth HARD.

Wasn't worth it.

I turned to leave.

Best I had at that point was, "Fuck both of you!"

I walked out, still shaking, ears ringing. He chose discretion and kept quiet as I left. She kept it up. In part, I think it was genuine, but also to play up the victim card.

"Baby, it's not what you think, let me explain, give me a chance."

I heard him mumble to her, "Just let him go."

As I backed out of the driveway, Jess stood in the doorway, now just watching, shaking her head. For the first time, I think- in all the time I had known her - she had nothing to say.

My head was spinning, I mean in one day, hell, in 12 hours, from Steve to the hospital, possible rape, to Mr. Cole, I couldn't get a grip on it. Yet again, I felt utterly betrayed, and, yet again,

I set myself up for it.

I have since come to understand another truth; you can never completely trust anyone. Given a particular circumstance and a specific set of dynamics, anyone is capable of anything. Don't be surprised, don't take it personally. Don't expect anything from anybody, especially a behavior. You will never be disappointed.

Now that may sound like a bad thing, jaded even, but frankly, it's not. The only person I can ultimately know is me (and even that's not an absolute). That is my one standard frame of reference. That being said, I must also accept that people get to be who they are and to do what they do. The only part I play in their actions is how I react.

That's just a harsh reality.

Took her a few hours for her to start calling, apparently giving me time to "cool down." She might as well have waited a month.

I was done, at least for now, I just couldn't take it. I blocked her number, and that was that.

Now in staying true to form to myself, I already had someone on the backburner.

I had been seeing someone off and on as well, mainly on the weekends. I had met her one weekend. I was on my way to see my soon to be ex-wife. She was a simple, sweet country girl, lived on a dirt road in a trailer. When Jess decided we were gonna go for it, I slowed things down. Well, the fact she lived two hours away didn't hurt, so, yeah. I was still seeing her. I justified it because I knew Jess was tricking, so that made it okay. Remember what I said about not trusting anyone? Yeah, that applies double to me.

Truth is: both of those women thought they were exclusive. The other reality is, I was a liar and a cheat.

I hadn't heard from Jess. She crossed my mind often, but I was hurt; moreover, I was angry. Maybe that's why I decided to see a girl who was the polar opposite of Jessica. Very sweet, not very well educated, country as country could be, much more voluptuous then Jess. I can honestly say it wasn't a conscious decision, but the evidence remains.

Either way, I had my little trailer park girl, she didn't think, and I didn't fall in love, it worked out just fine!

I was enjoying myself.

That is to say, I WAS, until one weekend when she stayed the night with me.

I woke up at 2am to yelling. Trailer park (TP) ran into the bedroom, "So who is this fucking n#$@%r banging on your door!?!? She says she's your girlfriend!!"

I wasn't quite awake until I heard that, then I was wide awake.

I ran into the living room and could hear Jess banging on the door, screaming.

"Who the fuck is this little bitch?? You motherfucker!! Let me in! I will beat her little cracker ass! Fuck her!!"

I didn't say a word, I was freaked out, TP asked in a whisper, "is that true?? Is that your girlfriend??"

"NO!! we were dating, but she was fucking cheating on me, so, no, we aren't seeing each other!"

Jess heard that. "THAT'S BULLSHIT!! We didn't break up!! You never said that!!"

I still didn't say anything. But in my head, I was thinking: technically, she was right, I didn't actually say we were split, but God damn, it should have been understood!!

I could see Jess looking through the blinds, then she started in on me.

"I can see your sorry ass standing there like fucking fool. You little bitch! Look, Tim, you kick that that little bitch out, she don't mean shit to you, I put in the time, baby, you're just mad, I get it, she's just some-thing to do. Put that little bitch out, Come on, Tim, let me in."

TP, completely taken aback by all of that, didn't have a clue what to do. She suddenly yelled through the closed door, "You're a whore!!"

Jess stopped dead, it got very quiet, I couldn't see much, but I could see that sick little smile cross her face and her voice calmed down, With a seductive lilt, she purred, "Oh that's ok baby, I'm sorry, what's your name Honey? Tell you what, you just open the door, let's talk, we'll have us a nice little chat."

Now THAT shit was scary.

Staring her straight in the eye, I told TP, "Whatever you do, don't open that fucking door!"

Jess was done. "Fuck you then, Tim!! I've been seeing a girl anyway!! You ain't shit!! You kick her little ass out and let me in, and everything will work out. You just mad, baby, I know, I understand, it's ok. I belong in there, I put in 4 fucking years, now you let this little bitch sleep in my fucking bed?? THAT SHOULD BE ME!! You know it! ME, not her! Look, I promise I won't hurt her, just put her out, and we'll call it even."

I hated it. I knew she was right, in my heart, but I couldn't, I didn't trust her at all. The second that door opened, she would have beaten the brakes off this little country girl, and then, well, then who the fuck knew, so, I told Jess I had called the cops.

"Ok, ok, I feel ya, alright then, Imma tell you some good shit. You fucked up now, you gonna be sorry, you fuck boy, you shouldn't add people into our story, they are just gonna get hurt."

She had started walking away when I heard a loud crash and then laughter.

I already knew what it was immediately. She had thrown her beer bottle thru the back window of my Durango.

The next morning, after explaining (and lying) about the nature of my and Jess's relationship and having to file a police report. TP and I headed down to the city hall to file a restraining order, a request TP made of me so that she could feel safe, and I could continue to get laid. I ended the weekend by filing a restraining order and a trespass warrant.

Didn't hear from Jess for a week or so, eventually got a call from an odd number; it was Jess. She opened with, "How's your little white trash whore?"

"Back in her trailer at present. How's your pimp?"

She just laughed. Yet again, our snappy repartee had begun.

It was odd; somehow, it felt like a weight had been lifted, neither worried about pissing the other off or what the other would say. It was different.

She told me she was living with a girl she had met at a convenience store, Rachael. Further, she was now wholly "adored."

I told her she deserved it, and I hoped she was happy.

That's the first time she said it, "I'm happy, but we both know we belong together. These are just poor substitutes."

Poor substitutes.

The pragmatic in me came out, "You might be right, Jess, we may end up together, but it won't be right now."

"Baby, I'm happy right where I am."

Again, ouch. A Jess zinger. Yes, I was jealous. I can't lie.

Before, I was everything to Jess (or so she said), and now I was on the sideline, but what was the alternative?

She asked about my upcoming show; How was training? Would I be ready?

I told her I felt good about it.

She said, "Well, you oughta do well, you look like a goddamn living GI Joe Doll."

We both laughed... laughed.

The pressure was gone. We could joke, we could laugh at each other, at ourselves.

Maybe this was the "right" thing to do.

Maybe this was the way we found our way back.

The phoenix must burn to be reborn.

SECOND CHANCE

Sometimes the only way to move forward is to take a
few steps back.

Second Chance

Shinedown

While Jessica and I were on hiatus, my business started blowing
up! Suddenly we had billboards and advertising all over town,
and I had become a sort of local celebrity. TP and I saw each other every
weekend. Generally, I would make the drive. It was a break from the
daily grind of work and got me out of town.

The restraining order and trespass warrant were still in place, and
the charges were still pending for my window, regardless. Jess and I
spoke often. A bit off, I know, but Jess had been in so much trouble with
the law she was just immune to it, and to be real, I only made those
moves to placate TP.

We kept it light for the most part, but there were always little jabs
here and there to keep each other on our toes. Amazingly, though, no

real blow-ups. She had taken on an oddly maternal demeanor and, quite frankly, it suited her. I had seen a glimpse of this trait years before.

While on maneuvers one night, she called and kept me on the line as she served up the drug du jour. While going through her usual patter, she suddenly stopped. I heard it all very clearly. The actual conversation isn't as crucial as are her reactions. Those spoke volumes: "You in that room, right? What the fuck you doing? You got kids in that room, right? Your kids? So where you gonna smoke this? FUCK, no, you're not!! You fuckin lost your goddam mind, girl! Get the fuck outta here, you ain't doin that shit on my watch. Go take care of your kids! Love em! Fuck this shit! I gave up my kids just so I wouldn't have to put them through shit like that, I'll be damned if imma let you do it right in front of me!"

She shut the girl down, would not allow it, even at the expense of missing out on a sale. Jess had her own kids taken away. Her narrative was that she surrendered her children willingly, to save them from the perils of her addiction. Make no mistake, she didn't give them up. They were taken away from her but that protective nature she demonstrated almost seemed born from that experience. As if she had lost the ability to do right by her own, so she took it upon herself to protect others from the same fate. It was admirable. This wasn't seen on the street, especially by those dealing.

One of the many dualities of Jess.

She was very excited about my upcoming show. She had taken it upon herself to help coach me. Well, maybe not formally but, she was constantly reminding me, "Don't you be cheating on your diet, I'm keepin' my fuckin eyes on you."

She followed up with, "You training like you should be? Seems like you're slacking up; you don't want me to kick that ass do ya?"

This was all very new, her being so involved, invested, to some degree, in my life. I liked it. I reciprocated, asked how she was, but all I got were Bambi and butterfly responses.

"I am adored. I cook for her every night, we have little parties, I dance for her, she lets me come to work with her..."

I would tell her that I was happy for her and that she deserved it, but

I knew many of these were digs at me. She tried her best to paint the pretty picture, but invariably I would get late-night calls.

"I just saw yo mother-fuckin billboard!! You gotta mother-fucking billboard! THAT'S MY FUCKING DOG!! I'M SO PROUD OF YOU!! THAT'S WHAT I'M TALKIN ABOUT!! THAT'S IS MY MOTHER-FUCKIN DOG!! I KNEW YOU WAS GONNA MAKE IT BABY!!"

She was so proud, honestly, legitimately proud, and it filled my heart. It was a rarity to see Jess so happy, so it really made me feel good when she was. To her credit, at her best, Jess could build you up so high you could see the earth's curve. Rest assured, even in this case, it wasn't done solely for that reason. As she kept going on and on, I could hear Rachael screaming at her in the background, "Fuck that mother fucker!! You like that motherfucker so much go be with him!! Oh, wait! That's right. That bitch won't even let you in his fucking house!!"

"Shut the fuck, Rachael!! You just jealous, bitch, you so fucking stupid!! This bitch going a 100 miles per hour swerving all over the fucking road!! Go ahead bitch kill us both!! You so fucking stupid!!"

Not the Bambi and butterfly scenario she had been painting. On the one hand, I loved hearing Jess being so proud of me, so happy, and on the other, again, being 1000, it didn't bother me to hear that things weren't quite the way she had portrayed them.

She kept me on the phone, just like always. I could hear them going back and forth.

Jess was comical, and Rachael? Well, Rachael just sounded drunk and pissed off. Eventually, we were disconnected. I found out the following day Rachael had slapped the phone out of her hand.

I was a week or two out from my show when Jess asked if she could help. Help? I couldn't figure out in what respect she thought she could help. Come to find out, "help" meant accompany me to the show. Yeah, I didn't see that as a great idea, tied at the hip for 3 days? I could see it going well, I mean, it could happen, but I could also see it how it could be a horrible idea. The whole risk-reward thing was pretty fucking skewed to one side. Besides, I had already asked TP to go. Again, because

I'm an idiot, I relayed that to Jess. Though we weren't technically together, it didn't go over well.

"Now that's fucked up!! We been seeing each other 4 motherfucking years, and not one time did you ever ask me to go to one of your shows!! Now, this little cracker ass 'ho shows up, and you take her!?!? That's some fuck-shit right there!! You need to fucking take me!! You at least owe me that shit!!"

Owe her? I owed her?? Somehow, forgotten was the fucking pimp and call girl scenario that had just played out, you know, WHY WE WERE WHERE WE WERE, but somehow I owed her? What the fuck??

I was trying to spare her feelings, "Jess, we aren't seeing each other, and even when we were, you were just too fucking volatile. Shows aren't vacations; it's work and stressful enough on their own, it would ruin me if you showed your ass at one!"

"I can behave myself when I need to, ya know? You have always underestimated me!!" She snapped back.

This had been a civil discussion thus far, and I didn't want to turn it into a Jess bashing session. As hard as it may be to believe Jess really WAS sensitive, so I offered, "Jess, I have no doubt you can behave yourself, but it's a chance I can't take. These are serious to me."

She still wasn't happy. She went with cutesy and in her best little pouty voice came back with, "How do you know if you don't give me a chance? You afraid we might have fun?"

I wanted Jessica in my life, though, I still had no idea how to make that work, but I did know that this wasn't even close to the right time. We were on a break, both seeing other people. This just wasn't going to happen.

"Jessica, I love you, but this just isn't where we are. You know this! You are with Rachael, and I am with TP. This is not the time for this."

"You know they're just poor substitutes. WE belong together. I am going to have my happily ever after."

There it was again "poor substitutes." She was right, again, tugging at my heartstrings, knowing exactly what she was doing. Things were going really well, and I didn't want to see things get back to where they were, but, again, I didn't want to beat her up or make her feel like I didn't care; I told her I'd think about it, that nothing was set in stone. It soothed her at that moment, and that was all I could ask.

The pressure increased as the show drew closer. Fortunately, I had something to serve as a much-needed distraction; My business was sponsoring a bikini contest at a local bar. I was one of the judges.

Now this one I was going to enjoy; I figured that Jess would get all bent out of shape when I shared that little nugget with her.

I called her up the night before the contest, playing it very nonchalantly. We exchanged the usual pleasantries, then I asked her what her plans were for the weekend. She said Rachael and her were going out of town for a little get-away.

I was like "cool, cool."

She asked, "What are you and your little dirt road hoe doing?"

Setting it up, I said, "Oh, I'm not seeing her this weekend."

To which I got "Oh my God! Are you already fuckin somebody else??"

I said, "No, no, we are sponsoring a bikini contest at a local bar, and I'm one of the judges!"

She hesitated for a second, but all I got back was, "Your business is sponsoring it?? Cool! That's what's up!!"

How anticlimactic was that?? I expected some huffing and puffing at minimum a little ruffling, but she was legit simply impressed that we were sponsoring it. Further, it made sense that I was a judge.

I tried to chide her a little with, "Maybe I can get one of the girls to try and influence my vote."

Suddenly Ms. Fairplay jumped in, "Fuck that, you just do the right thing motherfucker, and don't get any ideas about drinking or fucking up before your show either. I'll come right down there and slap the shit out of you!"

I reminded her, "Didn't say you and ya girl were going to be out of town for the weekend?"

Owning up, she laughed, "I was just trying to piss you off, I'll be here to keep an eye on you, I'll be checking."

This new wrinkle was charming, caring; inside my head, a little voice had an idea; maybe you should take her to the show!

What?!? STOP!!

Why? Because that voice is usually a complete idiot.

Let's just see how that could play out, upside vs. downside:

Upside is simple; we have a good time.

Downside, not so much, being; she shows her ass at the show, for whatever reason, causes a scene, gets fucked up, beats the shit out of somebody, goes back to the hotel, and sets the room on fire!!

I mean, really, what could go wrong?

After all, she and I had been through, I never ceased to amaze myself at just how blind I could be when it came to Jess. When your heart genuinely wants something, it tends to cancel out all logic and reason. Remember, when my friend told me, "The heart wants what the heart wants."?

Truth 1000.

Fortunately, in this case, I came to my senses quickly and, luckily, she never brought it up, so I was off the hook.

The night of the contest came. There I was camped out at the judge's table doing my best Judge thing. Jess called me every 10 minutes to "check" on me. Because I could hear Rachael screaming in the background every time she called, it wasn't hard to figure out her real motivation. Pushing buttons, creating drama, no, chaos. Chaos was the word. I finally had come to understand that Jess grew up in and had lived in chaos for so long she didn't know anything else. It was her natural environment. She strove to manifest it anywhere she went; It was her comfort zone. In the chaos, she created Jess swam like a fish in the water.

Peak week was upon me. Peak week: the dreaded 7 days before a show. Preparing the body to look it's best under the bright lights. Food is minimal. Training is grueling—each workout is designed to deplete all glycogen from the muscles. Sore, hungry, tired, suffice it to say you're not in the best of moods. Jess was calling several times a day to plead her case, but my resolve was unchanged.

Make no mistake, I wanted to just break down and take her. Ever hopeful, I knew she was expecting me to do just that, but she had taught me better over the years, and I didn't budge. TP and I left on Friday, made the 2-hour drive, Jessica calling and texting the whole time. Eventually, I was forced to block her number, just too disruptive to my mindset and challenging to explain to TP. We made it to the hotel and checked in, then off to the venue to register for the show. When I could get some separation from TP, I would unblock Jess and give her a quick rundown of what was happening. She was angry, mocking TP and bragging about what a great weekend she was planning for her and Rachael. I didn't bite. I gave her a brief report and then hung up.

As they do, the show came and went, 18 weeks of prep equal 5 minutes on stage if you're lucky. I placed well, first in my class. TP had a blast, looking at all the bikini girls, talking about competing one day. Shows tend to bring the competitive side out in people. We went for the usual food debauchery at one of the local bar and grills. It was deafening, which worked in my favor, as I had promised to tell Jess how I did. TP was about half drunk and wandered off to the bathroom. I made my call. Jess answered immediately,"It's about fucking time, just gonna leave a bitch hangin!! Soooo....How'd you do?"

I played it off a little to start, "Well, it was a stacked class, like 15 guys, so...."

She wasn't buying it, not for a second.'

"SO, your ass won?!?"

Yeah, she busted me.

"Yes, ma'am, first place in my class!!"

"HOLY SHIT!! FOR REAL?!?! THAT'S MY FUCKING DOG!! I KNEW YOU WOULD DO IT!! I KNEW IT THE WHOLE FUCKING TIME!!! THAT'S MY FUCKING MAN RIGHT THERE!! DAMN RIGHT!!"

Again, her exuberance was contagious. She could make you feel like you won the Olympia!!

She continued with, "So what's next? It's that real big show next, right? The one in Pittsburg?? Your ass is taking ME to that one!! Fuck that dirt road, ho!! I'm the motherfucker going to that one!!"

I could still hear Rachael screaming at

us, "You want her? Come get her ass motherfucker!! Love her!! Let's see how long that lasts!!"

Jess was screaming back at her to shut the fuck up and round and round it went.

I hung up abruptly when TP came back, immediately asking who I was talking to.

"My peeps, everybody wondering how I did."

Even then, I remember thinking just how slimy the scenario was, me hiding around corners to call my ex. Lying to TP, avoiding the subject. Sneaky and slimy, that's cheating—no other way to put it. How you come out of that and, in any way, feel good about yourself is still a mystery to me.

Jess kept calling, and yet again, I had to block her number until I could speak freely. I mean, it would not have been so bad if the dynamics were just a bit different, but they weren't. The fact was that I was sneaking around behind TP's back to talk to my ex, an ex that I had just recently filed a restraining order and trespass warrant against - not to mention filed charges for criminal mischief. There was no extenuating circumstance that could have justified even a piece of my behavior on either side of the equation. Yet there I was, sneaky and slimy, once again.

There is a behavioral oddity in some of us I have begun to recognize: It's not simply a Schlep-rock quality or a pull toward the darkness. That inherent nature to fuck things up. To hurt people through selfish action. Many of us have that; instead, it seems that there two sides to the quality; namely, some embrace that nature, sans conscience, either with indifference or a sick fascination of it. While others despise that intrinsic part of their nature, they feel the hurt they cause. They are repelled by it, but still, somehow, unable to stop it, powerless, only able to watch the oncoming train wreck.

Many years ago, I was cutting down trees to keep them from falling on a cabin that had belonged to my father, having no experience whatsoever. Most fell away from the cabin, but a few fell toward it. One, in particular, a larger one, hit the house directly. This cabin was precious to me, a final gift from my father. As I finished a cut, the tree started toward the house, the phrase, 'I immediately regret this decision' comes to mind. It started slowly. I saw what it was doing and attempted to push it away, to divert it, to change the course of what I had started. I braced myself at the base and tried as best I could, but it kept coming, as if in slow motion. My mind sped up, as did the falling tree, looking for a solution; I tried to push it to the side, but it still wouldn't budge.

I tried as hard as I could to find a solution, even if only to soften the blow, but there was just no stopping it. There was nothing I could do to stop it once in motion, no way to change its course. Once the cut was made, the die was cast, and nothing would change the outcome.

Einfühlung. This is what it feels like, that feeling of powerlessness, inevitability. That is what it's like to be one of "those" people, the ones who feel it, the ones who hurt from it, yet, somehow, are unable to stop the pain or the suffering we bring to the people in our lives. We see it starting, we recognize it, we even know that we will suffer in this as well, but, again, we cannot do anything about it.

Something in us is broken.

WHO WANTS TO LIVE FOREVER?

Everything is temporary. To try stretch a moment out, past its given time can only go one direction. When you finish this, sit quietly and listen

Who Wants to Live Forever

Queen

I t was Sunday night.

I had been working and training all day. I was just starting to kick back, getting ready to cook some dinner when I got a call from Jess, screaming and yelling. Her and Rachael were at it again. She pleaded with me to come to get her.

Specifically, she said, "Come get me before I kill this bitch!!"

Given our history, when Jess said shit like that, I listened. I jumped in my truck and drove to get her. Rachael lived right across the street from me. Knowing Jess and her ability to manipulate the dynamics of a situation, I always found it oddly coincidental that this girl that she had "just" met lived on the same side of town and less than a mile from my house. When I got there, she was already headed out the door with 2 clothes baskets, full. I saw that and immediately said, "What are you doing, Jess?? You're not moving in?!"

She came back with, "I just gotta get my shit outta here, so this bitch doesn't fuck it up."

Rachael was screaming at her from the front door, "Get your nasty shit outta my house, you fucking crack whore!! Fuck you!! You ain't nothing but a fuckin ho!! Yo pussy wasn't even that goddamn good anyway!!"

She and Jess continued to go back and forth, my head would flip back and forth as though I had a front-row seat to some verbal, profane tennis match. Jess went back inside and came out with another 2 baskets.

As she tossed them in my car, Rachael ran up to the passenger side window and started screaming at me, "Fuck you motherfucker!"

Now, without fail, there were a few things you really couldn't do around Jessica. A huge one was to disrespect one of her people.

Jess quietly but directly said, "Rachael, you better back the fuck up and shut the fuck up!"

But Rachael, quite ill-advised, continued, "Get your sorry ass outta here motherfucker, Fuck you and the horse you rode in on!!"

And the horse I rode in on??

I sat there and stared at her. I hadn't heard that line in 20 years, I thought it was hilarious. The fact that she stood there, as drunk as she was, and got it all out at once really impressed me. Jess had had enough. Rachael had her head and one shoulder in the passenger side window. I saw one of Jessica's hands grab her by the top of her head and the other by her throat. She yanked Rachael out of the window by her head and spun her around until Rachael started losing her balance. Once her balance faltered, Jessica spiked her head, face-first on the concrete. Rachael didn't move.

She just laid there, Jessica screaming over her. "That's what you get bitch!! What did I tell you?? You don't talk to my dog like that, fuck you!!"

I wasn't sure how bad Rachael was hurt, and I wasn't hanging around to find out. I yelled at Jess, "Time to go, Jess, got to go, got to go!! We need to get out of here!"

"Ratchet ass ho, fuck her!!"

Jess got in the car and off we went. She was still activated as hell, laughing about fucking up Rachael, "Did you see that stupid bitch? I told her to back the fuck off, I told her some good shit, shoulda listened, now you all fucked up!!"

I was quiet, a bit in shock. Jess was still reveling in her victory, but I was still reliving how quickly everything went next level. Jessica's ferocity never ceased to amaze me. But, again, things most always escalated quickly with Jess - Any semblance of balance was what she passed while swinging from one extreme to the other.

We got to the house and went inside. I, again, reminded her that she wasn't moving in. I was fortunate that my son was staying with his mom that evening. Brad knew of Jess but was not a fan. He only saw the effect she had on me. Most times, it wasn't good but to be fair, he really only saw the fights and extremes. He really wasn't around to see the better side of Jessica.

She started calming down, and I asked her if she was hungry. I had already been cooking for myself before she called, so I continued. I grilled her a steak and made some mashed potatoes. She loved it. Jessica loved food; it was indeed was a passion of hers. I learned much later, from Annie, that she had planned on going to culinary school at one point, further explaining our connection.

She was still going on about kicking Rachael's ass, her own physical superiority. She really enjoyed having that edge over other women. It was a fascinating facet of her personality. She had once told me when I asked her what her preference was, men or women, she said she loved sex with women, by far her favorite, but hated relationships with women. She said they were too clingy and didn't like sleeping in the same bed because it was too close, too intimate. Now she wanted relationships with men, because, she said, she felt a level of security with them. It always made me laugh because as much as she told me how she hated sleeping with women (actually sleeping) on the rare occasions I

WOULD let her spend the night with me, she would sleep in my bed and literally curl up around my head, sucking her thumb. It was incredibly precious to me, this badass, this killer of killers, wrapped up like a kitten and sucking her thumb, Yet another duality.

It was getting late, and I had to be up bright and early, so I settled her in on the couch, blanket, and pillow included. She asked about sleeping with me. I just reminded her of where we had just come. It wasn't that I didn't want her with me. For once, I just wanted to try and do the right thing by her, no expectation, no conditions. I went to bed, locked the door. I knew she wouldn't just take no for an answer. 30 minutes later, I heard her try the doorknob. True to form, as always.

She was crashed on the couch when I got up, Bren was curled up with her. She looked so peaceful, I loved watching her sleep. It was a rarity, but when she did, she slept HARD! I loved it. The dichotomy of this beast becoming the cuddly little kitten curled up on the couch. I told her I was going to work, and to please respect my privacy. Of course, I still locked my bedroom door, just to make things a little more challenging. I left her $20 and told her there was plenty of food in the fridge.

The whole time I was at work, I was concerned. The thought of her being in the house alone kept bouncing around in my head. Jessica did not have a good track record when it came to others personal effects. I remembered when she stayed in Crawfordville for a short time, she and a friend pawned off anything of value in a gentleman's place where they were staying. I also remembered her blowup at Steve's and destroying his entire house. Knowing the way that the whole incident played out kept me on edge the entire day. For me, everything had to be kept very secretive. I couldn't let anyone know she was at the house. After all, we had just recently been through, I couldn't have imagined what they would have thought. Those thoughts, those secrets, the things left unvoiced, those were the things that always left us vulnerable. My own arrogance put both of us in jeopardy, my lack of foresight condemned us.

I called to check on Jess several times throughout the day. Though I could not be sure, it seemed she had stayed put for the most part, still tired from the weekend, recharging. She had to have left because when I got home, she had her new fav Lime-a-Rita beverages, at the house. Jess owned no means of transportation, but she ALWAYS had a ride. As usual, I just didn't ask. I did that a lot with Jessica. Being a recovering addict, I was aware of the short leash addiction keeps us on. I also understood that when we are in active addiction, we are resourceful beyond belief.

Jess always, without fail, did what she had to, to assure she had what she needed. I just had learned to accept certain realities; one being Jess was going to do what she was going to do, I wasn't going to pay for her drugs, so she always worked it out. Truth be told, I'm not sure I so much accepted it as I simply used my forgetter (forgetter =an organ that addicts are born with that grants them the ability to erase all memory of just how ugly the life of addiction could get). In other words, I kept a short memory, maybe even a hint of denial in there. Whatever it was, for some reason, Jessica almost always got a free pass. As I walked in, there was Jess, sipping one of her drinks. Here was that slippery slope, Jessica had to have some alcohol or start having withdrawals. Having seen her detox those many times before, I knew how horrible it could be. It wasn't pretty. The trick was though, you had to make sure she didn't go over the edge with it.

This night was a good night. She just kept it at a maintenance level. She was very playful, funny, the best of Jess. I cooked dinner again, another steak night. When she was like that, I was utterly in love with her. I wanted time to halt so she and I could spend an eternity at that moment. This, I still choose to believe, was the real Jessica. It was the pendulum that always did us in. It was time to go to bed again. Jess had behaved herself for two days straight, unbelievable! I made sure she was comfortable on the couch. She said she was fine but had to throw in, "be happier in the bed" with her little scandalous smile, she never passed an opportunity for a little zinger.

I went to bed, locked the door again. I could hear Jess; she was up and down, talking on her phone, going outside to smoke, coming back inside, checking my door. She was restless.

The next morning started very much the same. She and Bren were bagged out on the couch again, cute as can be. I made my coffee told her there was plenty of food, locked my bedroom door, gave her a kiss on the head, and headed out.

Again, I stayed in touch with Jess on the reg. She was definitely recovered from the weekend and getting restless, ready for another run. She had gone out with Rachael for lunch. It always amazed me that Jessica would absolutely smash somebody then be out to lunch with them the next day like nothing happened. She had this magnetic draw to her, as crazy as she would get you liked being around her, like some fucked up train wreck, you kept watching, kept coming back for more, just to see what would happen next.

I stopped by and saw my son, he asked about all the clothes in my car, and I explained it was Jessica's. He wondered if she was at the house. I lied and said, "of course not," but he knew, everybody knew.

It's challenging to think back on those times, my dishonesty with my son, the people in my life, and mainly myself. Shit, I was lying to everybody. That's how it works; you don't want to hear everybody's disapproval, you already know what they are going to say, so you just lie and tell them what they want to hear. Reality is really just a matter of perspective. I got back to the house, Jess was still sipping. She had been in and out all day, but it seemed she hadn't crossed the line just yet. She was bragging about her day with Rachael. She loved to throw that in my face, letting me know how replaceable I was. Being honest, it did bother me to some degree, but I saw PT, and she knew it. Poor substitutes, right? We couldn't get it right as of yet, so we dated others as substitutes, poor ones at that.

It was undeniable that Jess and I were connected. I had fought it tooth and nail for as long as I could, but bottom line, year after year, there was always something. It was palpable. Neither of us was whole, neither of us could be in a healthy relationship, so we played this game, this dance, who cares the most, who cares the least, like some sick work of performance art.

I cooked dinner again. There was a tension that evening, posturing. She was drinking more and finding ways to "poke the bear," one of her favorite games. She would keep needling, pressing buttons until you finally reacted, then she would calmly say, "see, YOU have the problem."

Rachael came over, and Jess went outside to talk to her.

She came in a minute later and asked if she could take Bren out to show Rachael.

I declined.

Jess had stolen a dog once from me once before and took her all over creation. She opened the door and started yelling to Rachael about how nasty I was, how mean I was because I wouldn't let her take Bren. It was in those moments that Jess would cement her version of an individual in someone's mind. Jess was truly a master of manipulation. She set things up nicely, then she would steer you right into looking precisely as she had portrayed you when the opportunity arose. People would end up having opinions about others they had never met long before they ever met them and those opinions were always directed by whatever Jessica needed.

So yet again, I went to bed, locked my door, she tried the door several times that evening, restless, very restless.

The next morning, I was up before my alarm. I hadn't slept much. I heard her up and down all night, trying my door, talking on her phone, inside and outside. She was curled up with Bren again. Bren watched me as I made my way out the door, Jessica workin' that thumb.I made it a short day, concerned about Jessica's restlessness.

I got home and, as I feared, she was activated. She now had two cases of Lime-a-Ritas in the fridge and had obviously been working on them. I asked if she was ok, she said she was great, had got to see Rachael and was getting picked up by a "friend" to drop something off. She was jumpy, sketchy, I could tell she had the wheels turning. She left. I had to stay home; I damn sure wasn't giving her a key.

When she got back, she was even more shaky, very jumpy, didn't say much. Rachael pulled up a short time later. As Jess went out to talk to her, she had left her phone on the coffee table. Right, wrong, or indifferent I wanted to see what was going on so I picked up her phone and checked her messages. Gay Bob was the name I saw. First, she had been texting back and forth with him, her "friend," but there wasn't any talk about "dropping off." He talked about not being able to wait to "bust her pussy wide open" to "lick her up and down". He was a trick. She needed money, so she did what she did. It hurt, again, but this time, there was an element of humor. It was comical because Jessica couldn't stand being "caught". As a matter of fact, she hated it. It destroyed her illusions of control.

When she came in, I started on her. "So has anybody busted that pussy wide open today?", grinning from ear to ear, a complete ass. "Did it get licked up and down?? Gay Bob doesn't sound too gay…"

She just looked at me, wheels turning, trying to figure out, again, what I did and didn't know. I tossed her phone on the coffee table, "I'm surprised at you, Jess. VERY sloppy, you slippin'."

She wasn't amused. "You went through my phone?? YOU MOTH-ERFUCKER!! WHAT THE FUCK IS WRONG WITH YOU?? THAT'S NONE OF YOUR FUCKING BUSINESS! YOU DON'T EVEN KNOW WHAT ALL THAT IS!!"

Still, with my shit-eating grin, I said, "Well, it looked pretty self-explanatory, Jess. Trickin again?? Guess Rachael had the Ho part right, huh?"

She was losing it, coming apart, and I didn't give a fuck, but I too, was sloppy. I left my phone on the coffee table. She saw it and grabbed it.

"What if I go through your phone motherfucker, you fuckin bitch? Let's see who your slimy ass has been talking to, what about that?"

She tried to open it, but it was locked, now she was really going off. "GIMME THE FUCKING CODE MOTHERFUCKER!!"

She slung the door open and screamed at me, "I WILL THROW THIS MOTHERFUCKER RIGHT THROUGH YOUR FUCKING WINDSHIELD BITCH, GIMME THE FUCKING CODE!!"

I grabbed her phone, and calmly walked toward her.

"Here, let's just trade, I'll give you your shit, you give me mine."

I knew it was way too late for any reasonable solution, but I was trying to get close enough to grab my phone. She brought her arm back to throw, and I pinned it up against the wall. Jess immediately tried to head-butt me. She missed, just glancing off my shoulder. I got both hands on the phone and took it. As I pocketed my phone and turned to walk off, she punched me in the head, again, again. I turned back around and put my hands on her hips and drove her back. I pressed her hips to the wall and put my head in her diaphragm. This kept both of us safe. She had no leverage to wail on me. As I pressed her against the wall, something in my calf gave, a muscle tore, I immediately felt it.

I kept pressing, but was in a lot of pain. I asked her if she would stop, she said yes,

I said, "are you sure?"

"Yes! Yes, goddammit!! Let me fucking go!!" As I released her hips, she pushed me back and immediately kicked me square in my balls, throwing in a;

"Bitch ass motherfucker!!

I instinctively reacted, Pow, right in her jaw, not particularly hard, but a gut reaction from getting nailed in the balls like that. Her knees wobbled, and she dropped a bit. She looked up at me with her sick little smile and spit in my face. I limped over to the couch.

"Goddam Jess, I'm so sorry, but you can't just tee off on me like that and think I'm just gonna take it. Fuck!!"

"You're just like everybody else, nasty motherfucker!! You just hide that shit better than most, but I knew it would come out!!"

I hated it. Being grouped into the "everybody else" category. I didn't feel that was me, but who knows, maybe she was right. You stick around in that environment long enough, and that shit will change you, contagious, remember?

But I spun it around with, "You ever stop to think that maybe you just bring that shit out of people, babe?? I've seen it 100 times at this point."

She started sobbing, hard sobbing, "You just don't understand, it wasn't what you thought, he was just high, and I didn't want to fuck up his buzz, I didn't do anything…!"

How could it be anything other than what I thought, what I saw? But such was my madness, I WANTED so desperately to believe her that I tried to reason it into some form of reality. She was slapping her bare leg, repeatedly, with her hand, hard, like really hard, bringing the blood to the surface. I started asking her to stop, but she just hit harder. I began apologizing, me, to her, for HER fucking another guy? I was fucking crazy, *Follie au Deux* (shared psychosis), straight-up…. I was over the edge, we were over the edge, this was where things went completely sideways.

We talked for a while longer, she continued drinking, the scale was tipping. Once again, I made us dinner, but she wasn't hungry. She had other things going through her mind, bad things, bad intentions. Maybe if I had been in my right mind, I would have recognized the wave that was building, But I was oblivious, too self-absorbed, too arrogant, blind.

It was around 11:00pm, and I was getting tired. I cleaned up the kitchen and went to bed, but, for the first time, I didn't lock my door. I don't know why, can't say that I really even thought about it that particular evening, but sure as the sun shines, Jess began popping in and out.

She started with, "I'm glad you hurt your leg."

Other than that little zinger, she was just making cute jokes, being silly. Then she would disappear, I would hear the front door, and she'd be back, a little more activated each time. Finally, she popped in and cut on the light.

Now it was, "I need some money."

"Jess, its 2am. What in the fuck do you need money for?"

"I just got my period, I need tampons, for real, you wanna see??"

Now I knew she was lying, but I didn't feel like getting into a full-blown fight again, so I told her to grab some cash. My wallet was right there on the dresser. Not sure how much she took, but I'm quite sure tampons aren't quite as expensive as she seemed to think. Again, she left the house. I started to doze a bit when she popped back in, lights on, this time jumping in and lying in bed with me.

She started to cuddle up to me when I told her, "Baby, we both know this just isn't where we are right now. We both have our poor substitutes to deal with."

She agreed with, "I know."

She was climbing out of bed when it happened.

She saw a piece of rope on the floor, she wrinkled her face, and with a half-chuckle asked, "What the fuck is this?"

Staring at me for a straight answer. Her eyes demanding it. Well, I knew what it was and why it was there. Why I choose to tell her will always be a mystery to me. I mean, what the fuck was I thinking?? I tried to give her a laugh, "Well, MY poor substitute likes me to tie her up."

CLICK.

Jessica became unhinged, spitting profanities, she leaped on top of me. I was under the covers, so when she jumped on me, my arms were pinned, She started raining punches in on my face: 1, 2, 3, 4, 5, 6. All I could do was watch as they came in. My nose was bloodied, eye blackened, and she wasn't showing any signs of letting up. I managed to buck her up enough to get my feet on her and launched her off the bed. I shook off the covers and jumped up. She came straight back at me.

I kept trying to talk sense into her, to calm her down, but she was utterly gone; cursing, kicking, swinging wildly. I couldn't get a grip on her. Eventually, after a swing and a miss, I was able to bearhug her, she tried to duck out, and we ended up on the floor. It was a big sandwich, me on top, her underneath me and my arms under her. I couldn't get my arms out. I had her arms wrapped as well, but they were held down right at crotch level, and she took full advantage. She used both hands to start squeezing and twisting my nuts. I lost my breath, the pain was unbelievable, I couldn't even think much less do anything to get her hands off. I was completely reactive at this point.

Unable to do anything else and in intense pain, I bit down on her shoulder, hard. Eventually, I got my hands on hers. What I thought was pain was really nothing; trying to pull her hands off me was worse. I was hurt, head pounding, sick to my stomach. Eventually, I was able to stand up, She stayed down kicking up at me, she missed a kick, and I was able to throw her leg over so that her back was to me.

I secured a hand on her jeans skirt and immediately started dragging her out of the house, Jess kicking and screaming the whole time, "Ok ok,

I GOT YOU, I GOT SOMETHING GOOD FOR YOU MOTHER FUCKER, YEAH, ok, ok YOU GOT NO IDEA..."

This continued as I dragged her out of the bedroom. She was grabbing every piece of furniture along the way, creating a chaotic trail as she went. Eventually, we got to the door. I opened it and picked her up with both hands to throw her out. She grabbed the door frame to stop herself, so as she went out, so did it, the entire frame. She hit the ground and immediately scrambled back to her feet. I saw her coming, but my feet were wet with sweat, and the tile floor was slick, so I had trouble holding it shut. Her fingers came inside the door to pry it open. The minute I saw them, I grabbed two in my hand. I was about to break them, ANYONE else I would have snapped them, without hesitation. but, this was Jess. I didn't want to hurt her like that, so I released them. She backed up and ran straight into the door, she hit it full force, my feet slipped, and I fell back into my TV, wobbling it.

Now, as I have told this time and time again, re-lived it over and over, it became painfully clear just how oblivious I was. After all that she had already done, punching, kicking, twisting, after all that she had thrown at me, I turned my back on her to make sure I didn't knock my expensive TV over?

Seriously?

What a fucking idiot!! I recall it and have no idea what was going through my head. Nose bleeding, black eye, stomach aching from having my nut thoroughly abused, yet I was arrogant enough to simply turn my back to her to make sure my TV didn't fall.

Jessica was far too resourceful and too far gone to let that slide. I didn't realize it then, but she had secured a screwdriver from the window ledge. As I had my back to her, I never even noticed it. She resumed striking me in the back, puncturing me with every strike.

I didn't feel it, not once, didn't even notice. Small little dots in my back, the screwdriver was blunt, so, fortunately, it got very little penetration. I turned around and was able to grab her, again with the bearhug, but this time I turned my back to the wall with her back toward me, I squeezed her tight and said, "Are you gonna fucking calm down now?!?"

She didn't answer. In fact, she let out a sly little giggle. Even in all the commotion that concerned me, What was going on that I didn't know about? I looked down at my left leg, and there was a screwdriver being ground into my leg just above my knee.

That was the moment.

That was when I realized this was for real. This wasn't a typical Jessica temper tantrum.

This woman was trying to hurt me, badly, permanently.

Now I was starting to panic.

I threw her straight to the tile floor, put my knee on her neck, and used both hands trying to get that screwdriver out of hers.

I was a good 230lbs at the time, and I had all my weight on her, but she wouldn't release it. I hammered her hand on to the tile, and the screwdriver popped loose. I wasn't playing anymore, this had gotten very serious very quickly. I was wounded and done with the fucking games.

I slid down the wall and secured her in a rear-naked choke, Well, ok, that's what I thought it was, but discovered quickly that I had no clue what the fuck I was doing. We were both completely out of breath, gasping, she said, "let me go, let me go."

I complied. She wobbled up, scooping up the screwdriver on the way and tossing it at me. She staggered to the couch and took out her phone. I got up and staggered my way to the dinner table and plopped in a chair, facing her the whole time. She was on her phone, but I couldn't hear a word she was saying.

My ears were ringing, heart pumping, trying to catch my breath. I remember her saying "guns" or "gonna be guns," "waving around." I don't know, still not sure exactly what she said. She was passing the couch when she lost her balance and fell ass-first onto a glass coffee table. How she didn't just bust through it, I will never know.

She stood up and shuffled to the kitchen, opened up the fridge, and slammed two Lime-a-Ritas, one right after the other. As she turned toward me, she fell ass first again, this time, INTO the fridge, knocking out all of the shelves. She stood up and slammed another Lime-a-Rita.

She stood there, staring straight ahead for a moment. I sat and watched, wondering what was next. She opened the freezer, where I had a supply of GH and IGF, and started tossing the vials at me, hitting me in the head and chest. Not winging them, just being annoying as fuck. She stopped and again stared straight ahead, wheels turning, frighteningly so.

In hindsight, remembering, reliving the entire event, over and over. I fully believe that this was where she decided what she wanted to do. I had several guns in the house, basically one for each room. The thought being, if it ever became necessary to use a weapon, you needed one wherever you were in the house. Jess had apparently scoped out the apartment and located all of them. She made a beeline for the bookcase and took out my .357. By her body language, I could tell where she was headed. Almost simultaneously, we met there.

I took the gun and said, "Baby, we ain't taking it to that level."

I slammed it down hard on the table. Even at the time it seemed odd that she didn't fight or struggle for it. She simply let me take it. Slowly, I realized that she didn't plan on stopping there. She had made her way into the hallway and retrieved my 12-gauge hidden in the A/C closet. I heard her chamber a round as she came back around, quickly pointing the shotgun at my head, screaming, "FUCK WITH ME NOW MOTH-ERFUCKER!!"

I was lost. My mind didn't comprehend what was happening. How did this happen....? How did we get here?? What the fuck!! Regardless, there I was with Jess holding that shotgun to my head, screaming at me to look at her.

"LOOK AT ME MOTHERFUCKER, OH YOU GUNNA SEE THIS COMING, LOOK THE FUCK UP AT ME!!"

I kept my head down. I'm not going to lie: I was afraid to look up.

I would glance at the weapon, watching her finger ringing the trigger, pushing the catch to the fold-down stock. She started jabbing the shotgun barrel into my head, trying to get me to look, still screaming at me to look at her. Blood began streaming down my face. A huge knot had swelled up on my head from the repeated strikes.

I finally glanced up higher, just high enough to see her. I didn't know this person. Her face was contorted, her eyes were black.

Read that again. HER EYES WERE BLACK!!

Like some shit you'd see in a fucking movie, I had never seen anything like it before, and I pray I never see it again. My mind was returning. I began to think again, in those thoughts was a realization that this was it; she was going to blow my head off.

The next person who would come into this apartment would be my son. My own son would be the one to come in and find me, to see his father dead on the floor, with no fucking head......NO, this couldn't happen, not this way.

She struck me again, but this time I was able to swat at the muzzle. I knocked it out of her hand, but it fell to the side. She still had the pistol grip in her hand. I missed my chance; I was about to die. Instead, she threw down the shotgun. It hit the ground hard.

I remember being surprised that it didn't go off, even more so than she relinquished it. Months later, I found out the safety was on. What she thought was the safety was actual the catch for the fold-down stock. She would push it and then try the trigger. I saw her do it at the time but never realized what was going on.

She was trying to figure out how to make the weapon fire. She was trying to kill me.

When she dropped the gun, I hesitated, stunned as to why she would do that. Now I was really starting to think again, I had seen her run to the bedroom. I had a 9mm there. It was, under my pillow, full mag, one in the pipe. This one she knew about, but it was holstered tonight, it had been in my car earlier, and I never took it out of the holster. I grabbed the .357 off the table and limped to the bedroom. I was yelling at her the whole time to stop, to not do this.

She was frantically digging under the pillow, in a panic. I could see the holster, see her fumbling with it. I remember screaming at her, "Please baby, don't do this - Jessica!! Jessica, stop, stop, baby stop, please stop! DON'T DO THIS!!! Please!!"

She looked back at me, this person I did not know. Her eyes still completely black, her face twisted into this horrific half-smile, she started to turn toward me. I raised my arm, screaming, screaming at her to stop. Begging, "STOP!!! BABY DON'T, PLEASE!!"

Suddenly, two shots – bang, bang – one right after the other. They were muffled in the small room. I opened my eyes, it was me, I had fired two rounds.

To this day, I don't remember pulling the trigger, no recollection of willing my finger to pull the trigger. Somehow it just happened. After all the commotion, the screaming, the yelling, the fighting,

suddenly, it was deathly silent. Nothing. Not a sound. Only the ringing in my ears.

I slowly began to hear a low guttural moan through the ringing.

Time slowed down, everything slammed into slow motion. There was smoke—the acrid smell of gunpowder.

The whole surreal scene is burned into my mind forever.

Jessica slumped down on the bed now, her legs still moving, trying to speak, to breathe, I was numb, afraid to get closer to her. Somehow, I thought she might be playing possum, waiting for me to get closer. I started saying her name, "Jessica, Jessica? Baby?"

I came closer. I saw the pistol. It was beside her, still in the holster. The snap undone. I remember picking it up, getting it away from her, snapping it, then placing both guns on the dresser. It was robotic, mindless. Nothing felt real.

I continued saying her name, "Jess, Jess baby, you ok, talk, talk to me, please say something..."

I was close to her now, looking in her face. Her eyes were still completely dilated, black. She was staring straight down at the bed, eyes wide open, lips were moving, trying to speak, trying to breathe. Her breaths were short and fast.

I looked over her body, I saw a hole in her side, a small red star, like an asterisk, it looked so small...

"Jess, are you ok, babe? Baby, talk to me, please, can you hear me?"
Nothing…

She was fading, going away, lips blue, face paling. Suddenly there was a loud sound, like air escaping from a balloon. It was from the hole in her side. I couldn't have known then, but months later, I learned that both rounds wreaked havoc. Her lungs were destroyed. She couldn't breathe, it was impossible. The air was filling her chest cavity. Once the pressure was great enough, it escaped through the hole in her side.

I grabbed my phone and frantically tried to call 911. I couldn't fucking dial it, my hands were shaking too badly, eyes wouldn't focus. I must have tried 5 times. It seemed to take forever. Finally, I got it, "What is your emergency?"

The first hint of reality, the first time it slowly started to seep in, "I SHOT MY GIRLFRIEND!"

I remember that the rest is a blur, getting info, address, is she breathing? Conscious? Talking? "She's bleeding!! Bleeding badly!!"

The operator told me to apply pressure. I grabbed a towel and desperately tried to do as she asked. As I went to put the towel over the hole, more air came out, with it, dark, dark blood, with some sort of white material.

I started saying, "I don't know.... I don't know..." to the operator.

I was still trying to talk to her, "Jess, baby, can you hear me, please talk to me." I could see she was leaving, fading farther away, dying...

Not much time had passed, but it seemed like forever. I started yelling at the operator, "She's DYING!! Where are they!!! Why aren't they here?!??"

She said, "They're outside, you need to go tell them where she is."

I bolted to the front door.

That was the last time I ever saw Jessica.

I wish I had known. Done something. Said goodbye. Kissed her, something, anything.

But I did not.

I didn't know; how could you?

I ran out the front door. Cop cars, lights, sirens, yelling, guns were drawn pointing at me, "Don't move! Don't move! Let me see your hands!!! Hands up, hands up turn around!!"

I yelled, "Get in there!! Go help her!! She's in the bedroom!!"

They kept their weapons on me till I was cuffed, then walked me to a car.

I had just been in a fight for my life, then watched, helplessly, as my boo faded away...

Now I was sitting alone, handcuffed, in the back of a police car not knowing what was going on...

The truth is, I never left that room, not in any way that mattered. In fact, even now, I'm still there. The sights, the sounds, the smells, I see it every day, every night, some nights the whole night through. Burned into my mind, like a bright flash, burns a blue spot into your vision. No matter where you turn your gaze, it's there. The more intense the light, the longer it lasts. That whole night is my blue spot. The intensity so great, it never fades. Our relationship, all we went through, it was a candle burning brightly, intensely, from both ends. There was no way it could endure. It all culminated in that night. In an instant, my boo, my lobster was gone. No, happily ever after. No, remember when's.

No more chances.

Time caught up with us...

OLD SOULS

This was us. I want so badly to believe It, but it is so hard to hold on to this thought. Listen now.

Old Souls

Paul Williams

So, where do you go from here? Not long after, I was asking why, *WHY would you go from here?* Who the fuck wants to carry that shit around?

Well, I went straight to a police car. I sat Handcuffed in the back of that police car, alone, isolated. Occasionally, a cop would walk by, and I'd ask how she was. They just looked at me and kept walking. There was an ocean of police cars and one ambulance. Cars would come and go, but I noticed that a solitary ambulance wasn't moving.

Now, at this point, I wasn't sure of her condition. Well, maybe that's a lie, I don't know, perhaps I was in denial, I saw her, unable to speak, turning blue, but she was still breathing when I left, they got there quickly, maybe....I wouldn't allow myself to accept that she might be gone, much less because of me.

My nuts hurt, calf was throbbing, headache, black eye, huge knot on my head and dried blood on my face, I was topless and commando in loose black gym shorts. I must have been quite a sight. The ones that did pass by looked at me like I was some kind of freak, this big muscle-head bodybuilder who had just beat up and shot his girlfriend. I felt like they looked at me like I was a piece of shit. I'll never really know if what I interpreted as disdain was real, but I certainly remember how I felt.

I hadn't slept in over 24hrs, but I wasn't really tired. I was forcing myself to believe she wasn't gone, somehow, they fixed it, fixed her, but there that ambulance sat. They must have been in there doing their EMT shit, making things ok, stabilizing her.

When the ambulance slowly pulled out, no lights, no siren, the doubt crept in. No...she was stable, so they didn't have to hurry. It was still ok.

A female deputy came walking by again. I asked, "Is she ok?? How is she?" she just looked at me, expressionless, my heart sunk.

I was thinking, this can't be real, there's no way this is real, it's not happening, Jess will come bouncing out of there and kick me right square in the nuts again, just wait. Didn't happen.

What did happen was a long quiet ride to the Sheriff's office and then hour upon hour of questions. As they walked me in, they kept me cuffed the entire time, still no shirt, no shoes, limping, people looking at me like an animal in a cage. Perhaps the most uncomfortable I've ever been. They sat me in a small room with cameras and left.

A few minutes later, two detectives walked in, and I was asked to relate what happened.

"How is she??" was my response, and I asked it over and over and over.

"We should get a report soon."

They were stalling me, to keep me talking, feeding me bullshit, fucking BULLSHIT!!

So, question after question, asked in a variety of ways, "You're a big guy you couldn't handle her without shooting her" "why two shots?"

"why so many guns?" "Why did you follow her into the bedroom? Why not run?"

I told them everything, exactly as I remembered it, in as much detail as I could. They kept trying to find a loophole, a mistake, a change in my story. They had investigators in the apartment while I was being questioned.

Everything I told the detectives was relayed directly to the guys on scene to confirm what I was telling them. The fight, the screwdriver, the guns, I told the chaos to them precisely as I remembered it. For Christ's sake, it had JUST happened!! You fucks were there in 10 minutes!! You could still smell the fucking gunpowder. SHE WAS STILL ALIVE!!! HOW IS SHE?!?!

"I'm sorry, Mr. Durning, Jessica didn't make it."

All I could do was stare, the words he said, the words he used, and they didn't make sense. My mind couldn't fit them. I couldn't arrange them to form any semblance of something I could understand. Mouth open, eyes welling, I fell apart. At that moment, that singular moment, every-single-thing-in-my-life changed. My entire world went black.

Nothing was the same, NOTHING.

Every single thing, to this very day, has had a heaviness hanging over it. Somehow on that day, my life's gravity was altered. It became stronger, everything was heavier, making it hard to breathe, somedays hard to move.

I cried every day for a year. I didn't want to be here, I wanted her back... to be with her.

A DO-OVER!! YES!! That's what I wanted!! A DO-OVER!! I just wanted another chance. I Just wanted to say goodbye.

Was that too much to ask??

But our last goodbye was never said.

The detectives left and allowed me to compose myself before resuming their questioning. At this point, they were getting more insistent about things, pressing me. I was tired, exhausted. I was trying to hold myself together.

They came back in and asked, "You're a bodybuilder, right?"

Oh, my God. I stared at them with a "really?" face.

"Yes, I am a bodybuilder."

"We need to ask you about steroids."

Huh? Whisky Tango Foxtrot?

Halfway shaking my head, I replied, "What about steroids?"

The detective studied me now, watching how I responded, he asked,

"We need to know what you're on."

Somehow, I was able to come out with, "So, I've been up for almost 30 hours, you guys know everything that just happened, what we just went through and now, now you ask me this?"

"Exactly, Yes. We are asking you what you are on?"

This was taking an alarming turn. I didn't know exactly what they were doing, but I did know it wasn't good. I asked, "Is this where I need to get an attorney?"

To which I received, "You can do whatever you want, that's your right. But right now, you need to answer the question. We need to know what steroids you are taking."

Look, 1000, I am a competitive bodybuilder, a pro at this point. Yes, I have taken steroids, but that fact and this situation were mutually exclusive. I was getting the feeling that was NOT the direction they were going.

"I think I need to talk to an attorney."

"That's fine, but, one more time, what are you taking?"

"I want my attorney."

I was not under arrest at this point. I had not been read my rights. I had been detained and held in cuffs. When I attempted to exert my right to an attorney, I was illegally questioned. Ok, 1000, again, I knew none of that shit until my attorney got there.

I made a call to the only lawyer I knew: a food client.

Enter Ron Humphrey. They had left me alone in the room, still cuffed, until Ron got there. I had no experience with lawyers. I knew Ron through my business and a few in-depth conversations we had regarding food and training that was it. When Ron came in, he completely took over.

I have to say it was astounding: I was so tired, my thinking wasn't clear, had multiple injuries that were never addressed, and Ron came in and let them have it.

"Why are you, cuffed? Is my client under arrest? Has he been handcuffed the entire time? Has anyone addressed these injuries? Have they spoken to you since you requested an attorney? Have they asked if you need an ambulance? Where is your shirt? Can we at least get my client a shirt?"

Boom, boom, boom, genuinely nice, very polite, incredibly well-spoken, but very direct, and very to the point.

I was not holding up well. I would fall apart and break into tears. He sat with me, patiently, empathetically, he and his assistant. They cared. They were worried about me. At a point when my world had been destroyed, and I was utterly broken, it is not overstating it to say that Ron rescued me. Ron quite literally shut down his law practice to come in and represent me.

So, there we sat, the detectives would come in ask questions, Ron would advise me either to answer or not. They took blood, DNA, scrapings, they took pictures, pictures of everything- EVERYTHING! They were VERY thorough.

I was standing, naked, as they photographed my dick and balls (you know, where she grabbed and twisted) when one of the detectives off-handedly asked me to raise my hand as if I were going to fire a gun.

Ron jumped all over it, raising his voice for the first time, "Don't do that!! My client WILL DO NO SUCH THING, that is beyond ridiculous!"

He huffed. "Is my client under arrest??'"

"We haven't made that decision as of yet."

"Well, he hasn't slept in over 30 hours. I, for one, do not feel it is in my client's best interest to continue this. Shock and lack of sleep have left him impaired; he isn't under arrest, yet you left him handcuffed for hours, you haven't even offered medical attention."

He went back and forth with the detectives, some in front of me and some outside the room. He came in and sat again, waiting. When the detectives came back in, they asked if they could question me yet again. As tired as I was, I would have been ok with it; I was simply telling them what had happened, that's it.

Ron was NOT about to have it, "You have questioned my client, ad nauseam, for hours. Prior to council and subsequent to my arrival. In that time, you have not yet found reason to charge him. Emotionally, he is a mess. He needs time to rest and compose himself. He needs food, and he needs medical attention, which you neglected to offer him. Release him or charge him."

I heard the words but never made the connection. Charge him. Charge him? The stark reality of it all suddenly came over me; Charge me?? Murder?? But I wasn't trying to kill her. Never even crossed my mind. Did they not hear me? Did they not understand how I begged her to stop, pleaded with her to stop.

I never wanted to hurt her, I just didn't want to get shot, that's it, just didn't want to get shot. I didn't shoot to kill, I only fired so she wouldn't shoot me, I begged, I pleaded with her to stop- "PLEASE DON"T DO THIS!!"

But instead, I shot her. Two shots. My Boo, My lobster. She died, bottom line. Maybe all this was simply what was going to happen. Maybe, after it all came down, my life was about to be over too. I mean, I took her life, what would you expect?

Moments later, they came back. I was to be released. Again, Ron spoke with them and settled a few more things. He came in and quickly shot out, "Let's go."

Further explaining quietly,

"Don't look back, keep your head down, just keep walking."

As we got outside, he stopped and squared up on me, hands on my shoulders. He looked into my eyes, staring at me deeply, mean-ing/feeling what he was about to say, making sure I would feel it too: "I'm so sorry for what you went through. But you have got to know that you did what you had to do to be here now. I know you didn't want this; I know you loved her. I know. But Tim, I have seen these scenarios.

Most times, they go the other way. Make no mistake, she would have killed you. You are lucky to be here."

Lucky.

I didn't feel lucky. I have never felt lucky.

It's a tough thing to explain to someone, much less understand yourself.

I loved her, but I killed her.

I... killed... her...

Time has changed my perspective on many things, but "lucky" has not been a descriptive for which I have cared.

It is no small matter to take a life, especially when you have absolutely no intention, no thought, or want of taking. One that is precious to you. It's not like a movie or a video game, its physical, its intimate. It is permanent. You can take class after class after class to teach you how to protect yourself, what to do, how to do it, but no one tells you that the moment that weapon is fired, everything changes. It cannot be recalled. That there is another human being at the other end of that action and no, it's not a "bad day" or "gonna leave a mark," it's a violent, penetrative moment, leaving in its wake a human being struggling to stay here, fighting, gasping for one more moment, just one more second. Seeing that is a glimpse into an abyss wherein there is absolutely nothing looking back. This is where one begins to comprehend the fragility of life.

To take a life is just that, it's **taking** a life. You TAKE everything someone has, everything, every second, all they have done or will do. You have just stolen everything from them.

After all that had transpired, the insanity of the night - the fight, her death, the questioning, no sleep, no food - You walk out of the Sheriff's office and directly back into your life. Nothing outside has changed, the world is the same, but you are not, not at all.

Ron took me to the hospital. On the ride, he told me to get everything checked out, head, leg, bloodwork, anything that might help. He was very thorough, but I was not. Too tired, too broken, I couldn't focus on what he had asked or on anything else for that matter. He dropped me off and went back to his office. They took x-rays, checked the leg, checked my head. I cried the whole time, reliving it all over and over again. My mind was now an enemy, the pictures burned into it. I couldn't stay there any longer.

Ron had already called my son and ex-wife Lori to pick me up, so I left. I just limped out and waited in the parking garage. I sat alone with my thoughts, the movies still repeating, but now a new element had been added. I couldn't stop thinking about where Jessica was now, what they had done with her, with my Boo. Picturing her in a cold room, alone, cutting her open, it would hit me in waves, bringing me to my knees.

I needed this to stop; I was losing it quickly. I could literally feel my sanity slipping away; I could not stop the pictures, the intimate details, they raced through my mind. I could still see her eyes, smell the gunpowder, hear the ringing in my ears. I would start thinking; this is not real. She is ok. They are just separating us, just keeping us apart to get our stories, it's all going to be ok. She is ok.

Even writing this years later, the memories come flooding back in, the heart speeds up, the mind races, literally takes your breath. It's like a scalp wound. It only takes the smallest of nicks to open it up, and then the blood just pours out.

I heard a honk and looked up: Lori and my son, Brad, were there.

I saw them, but it was almost like looking at them from behind a sheet of glass. I mean, I was physically there, but I was also far far away. As though I was in flux, part still here and part still with her. We didn't really speak, I asked if they knew what happened, they said only what the police were allowed to tell them. Tim was angry, rightfully so, to have Jessica stay with me, I had him stay with his mom and her boyfriend. I lied to him. Not my best parenting job.

I mean, I had picked him up from school every day, but the four baskets full of Jessica's clothes in my car had already tipped him off to what the deal was. Lori was quiet. She just stared at me.

Lori was and still is my best friend; she is also an empath, so she wasn't just seeing me, she was feeling me. She has since explained to me that at that moment, she felt only a shell of my former self. But honestly, not even that - more like an exposed nerve that was feeling everything that had happened. Everything all at once, but no longer present in anyone's reality, not even my own.

It was embarrassing; I cried until I couldn't cry anymore, then I cried more.

I was done here, done.

I just wanted to be with her, that second chance, fuck everybody else. I was lost in a world without her. How did this happen? The world no longer made sense. My heart and soul were shattered, and somehow, she took some of those pieces with her as she left.

I didn't sleep for weeks, well, not at night anyway, I had to have the lights on, a TV on, I would play the same movie over and over and over. I had to have light because, in the darkness, I would see her face, swirling. I still felt her. She was somewhere else, lost, not able to find her way.

I was fucking nuts.

Thoughts scattered, riddled with guilt, absent from reality.

I remember telling my business partner, I could still feel her, see her, that I knew she was coming back to get me. He laughed

"No, no, she ain't, that ain't the way that works."

That was the best he had.

No one had a fucking clue. I couldn't turn it off. I couldn't get away. If I'd have had my gun, I would have blown my fucking head off in a heartbeat, just to not see and feel this shit anymore. I was floundering aimlessly.

Much later, my only catharsis was writing. It started slowly, just a sentence, a thought, usually on my phone. Eventually, a feeling would make it out.

Daily

I recognize it

Daily

The fact that I'm not ok

The fact that something

Deep inside

Has intrinsically changed

Thinking, feeling

It's all different now

All traced back to one moment,

one event,

The moment she left

Seeing her,

the empath in me

feeling her

Dying with her

In that moment

Something broke

A piece left with her

The piece that belonged to her

I don't know

The things in my head aren't right anymore

I pretend

Most people don't know,

They have no idea

I wear the mask of Thalia

People think it's me

But it's not

I don't know if I ever will be

The me I used to be

The me I knew

As time passes

Things do change

But change is not necessarily growth

In fact, it's not

It's Absence

Absence of us

Of what might have been.

That was really it. What might have been?

We never finished, no closure, we never even said goodbye for Christ's sake!

For the first year, I went to a therapist, a friend. Dr. Jan. I had seen Jan previously, after my mother's death, so we had some history. Jan was the best. She was immensely helpful, trying to help me forgive myself and somehow reconcile some of these feelings. This was such a horribly unique circumstance. There was no textbook for this. There were times I would spill my heart, and Jan would sit and listen, no words, no advice, she just sat and listened. In those moments, that was what I needed more than anything else—a safe place to pour out my soul. The thing was, trying to move forward felt like I was trying to finish a jigsaw puzzle with a piece missing.

How do you do that?

You don't, at some point, however long it takes, you to bite down and realize this is simply the way it is now, this is your world.

Part of me

No matter how I busy or distract myself,
sooner or later it catches up,
when it slows down
I start to catch my breath
The stark reality,
the blue spot on my soul
like a flashbulb leaves in your eyes,
but this doesn't fade
The pain and sadness continue,
Some moments
hard to breathe
I have quit asking

"will this ever go away?"

It won't,

nor should it,

it's supposed to hurt

to change you,

and so it comes to this,

if there is no end,

what is left?

In silent introspect and deep reflection.

I am left with one answer.......

Acceptance,

When all is exhausted,

Acceptance

the pain and loss are simply part of your life now,

good days

bad days,

but You will always remember

Our lives are fleeting

and we cannot change the past,

this is the truth of it,

this is the beginning.

Retrospect.

While it's a weird analogy, well, here it is: King Kong was exactly what he needed to be in his world. He had adapted to his dynamics and transcended his environment to become exactly what he needed to be to survive. Where it all got fucked up was when he was taken away from the world to which he had adapted. He didn't ask to be there and, as such, was unable to adapt quickly enough. He wasn't evil; he simply reacted to this new world as his evolution had molded him to do. Was it violent? Yes. Raw? Yes. Malicious? No. He only acted as his nature directed him.

He did not deserve to die for acting on his nature.

Jessica did not deserve to die either.

Too often, what we believe to be the best of intentions lead nowhere or to an utterly dead end. "When someone shows you who they are for the first time, believe them" again, Mia spoke the truth. When someone reveals their nature to you, recognize it, remember it, expect it. Take off your fucking rose-colored glasses and accept them for who they are, who they TOLD YOU they were through their actions. Not for who YOU WANT THEM TO BE. For those of us who fail to do this, well, be prepared to take ownership of everything that happens from that point on.

Jessica needed to hear that she had touched others, that she was deserving of love.

And I needed to tell her how much she meant to me.

I love you.

Baby, I still love you.

We were connected on a deeply emotional level.

We are still connected.

I cannot explain that statement.

I simply know it to be real.

Like Love.

Like God.

There is no tactile proof. You just know.

I have never actually seen the wind – but I have felt it.

I KNOW it is real.

MY IMMORTAL

It never goes away; all those "what ifs," the thousand questions, how things could have gone. At some point, you are forced to accept and move forward

My Immortal

Evanescence

R eal. The other part of being real is that…life goes on. 1000. That is real. Ever heard the saying that, "Every new beginning comes from some other beginnings end?"

While it is indeed true, it is also not that simple either. I never seemed to get that "new beginning" thing…fuck…I never even felt like I got the other beginning's end.

I never even went back to the apartment…never set another foot in it. That was the end of that place, for my son and I there…our little world. It has since become a sacred place to me. I still drive by…bowing my head, paying my most profound respects, and still seeing her.

A few weeks passed. I was downtown, and ran into the detective who had questioned me, Detective Hansen. He asked how I was.

I said, "I miss her."

He looked at me and slowly nodded, following up with, "Not many people make it back after something like that. Are you doing ok?"

I gave a halfhearted attempt at a smile and nodded, then asked, "Am I allowed to ask you a question?"

He looked a little puzzled at first; but then explained that his job was done, and that the sheriff's Dept had already closed the case...so I could ask him anything.

"What was she on?" I struggled to get the words out.

I need to relay though, "why" that question:

While waiting for an investigation, and the grand jury to do their work, you have zero contact with them. You don't "poke the bear," so to speak. That being said, you have a thousand questions to which you cannot get answers: What drugs was she on? Was the safety engaged on the shotgun? Did she have the pistol in her hand? Those questions will be answered in the police report, but they will drive you crazy up until then. I felt I could ask only one question, so I just wanted to know: "What she was on?"

I thought maybe that might help me to understand why it escalated to that level? What was different?

He just shook his head and looked at me again, "What wasn't she on, Mr. Durning?"

He listed a few of the drugs found in her system. Again, I could only nod...no words. We lingered in uncomfortable silence for a moment. I said thank you and walked away.

Six weeks after her death, the grand jury chose not to indict me, and they ruled Jessica's death a "justifiable homicide." You would know it as "self-defense." Those words meant extraordinarily little to me. They didn't bring her back...nor did they bring about any form of forgiveness. A year later, while going through some Facebook folders, I found a spam message folder. When I looked in the folder, there were no less than 30 messages from Annie, Jessica's biological mother. At first, I was afraid to look. When I did, I quickly saw I had every right to be cautious. The messages were precisely what one would expect: a grieving mother. It made sense. I read every one, each more painful than the other. I didn't know what to say, or what to do; but her last message made it clear... Annie was in pain. She couldn't get the answers she needed to find some peace. Paraphrased, she pled that I was the last to see Jessica alive, and how unfair it was that I wouldn't talk to her. All she had as her last memories of her daughter were of Jess on a cold slab, completely covered in sheets except for her face.

It crushed me, so I had to reach out. I made contact on Facebook first, kept it civil. I was cautious...scared. She texted to ask if we could speak. I agreed and gave her my number. When she called it was chilly between us initially (as one would expect), but then Annie said plainly, "I need you to tell me what happened. Step by step...every detail. I'll tell you right now that I knew my daughter very well. So if you are lying, I will know immediately."

Again, I agreed. With my voice shaking, I began relaying to her the entire experience–crying through much of it–reliving it all again. When I told her about Jessica's eyes–when I'd looked up and seen her blackened eyes–she stopped me and said, "I've seen that. I've seen her like that. It's called Bipolar rage. I'm sorry, Tim. I'm so sorry it had to come to that; but there was nothing you could have done at that point. I believe you did what you had to do."

Finally... I wasn't crazy. At long last, a confirmation that I had actually seen what I believed I had witnessed. I hadn't felt that anyone up to that point really comprehended what I was saying when I described Jessica's eyes. For instance, the detectives had looked at me like I was crazy when I described it. Many others were just being polite in accepting it. I was sobbing. To hear that from her meant more than any grand jury or law enforcement opinion. Annie is a devoted Christian, and as such, once she heard it from me directly...she forgave. I have no idea how. She asked if Jess had said anything...any last words. I said no– she tried, her mouth was moving–but she couldn't get anything out. She then asked the most painful question of all: "Do you think she suffered?"

Fuck. Ouch. I told her I talked to her the whole time; but Jess just stared down. I was there saying her name until I had to leave. "No, Annie...I don't think she suffered. I think she was too high to really know what was going on...I don't know."

The train of thought just hurt. It led to more and more questions. It was a thread I had purposefully chosen not to tug on up to that point. I do not know that I could forgive someone in the same circumstance; but somehow, Annie did. We stayed in touch, shared Jessica stories, laughed about her crazy self, and cried in missing her.

Back in my life, everyone had advice. Their words of wisdom. Please understand, I know that people just want to help; but after watching from a front-row seat while my mother died from pancreatic cancer, I have my own opinion on unsolicited advice of a "theoretical" nature... you can stick it up your ass.

People love to offer all sorts of ideas about everything "happening for a reason", "the power of prayer", "what it says in the Bible"...all sorts of shit.

IT IS OF NO SOLACE!!

Allow me to explain something.

I will preface it with this: My mother was a devoted Catholic. There was church every Sunday, and priests over for dinner. She had been a choir director, and played the organ for the church as well. When she had everyone praying over her, she shared with me that she believed that angels were coming down from heaven and taking the cancer out a piece at a time.

A month later, she was dead–starved to death–a horrible way to go. Why? Because if you get pancreatic cancer, you are going to die. I suggest getting your affairs in order and enjoying the living shit out of the time you have left. Now having been through that little shit party, I have very little tolerance for people who feel the need to explain how it all works. Especially when it's from people who have not experienced any of the "big" shit that life has to offer. In truth, their reaction to your suffering makes them uncomfortable, so they try to fix you in order to feel better themselves. That is not how it works. Let me sit quietly with my pain. If you choose to sit with me...feel free; but please, keep the Peter Pan advice. Until you have experienced a "big" trauma...the kind that bends your knees...shakes your very foundation...makes you question why the fuck you are even here, you truly have NO idea what you believe or don't believe. You THINK you do; but let me tell you, until life hands you one of those shit sandwiches (or worse)...you do not. It is then, and only then when you will find out what you DO or DO NOT know. When the rubber hits the road, THAT is when you can figure it out or not figure it out, because THAT is the only time you can. Nothing will prepare you because nothing CAN prepare you. You will get it when you get it. You will get no points for style (thank God). You will get through however you possibly can. By whatever means necessary. White knuckled, screaming and yelling, or praying on your knees...it makes no difference.

"No one can tell what goes on in between the person you were and the person you become. No one can chart that blue and lonely section of hell. There are no maps of the change. You just come out on the other side. Or you don't."

- Steven King

So...half in, half out...that's where I was, and that's where I stayed. Weeks, months, years all passed–stuck–unable to get out of my own way. The business was doing well enough that we attempted to expand to another city. I was the one who started the business, so I was the one to go. This meant leaving my home, my son, everything I knew. I lived out of a hotel room for almost 2 years. Coming home just on the weekends. I never told anyone; but, on the three-hour ride–alone with my thoughts–I would put my hand in the passenger seat and imagine holding her hand, like on our long rides together. I could almost feel her hand holding mine. I have had entire conversations with her.

Completely fucked in the head. Setting myself up. I was already failing. Failing in business, in relationships, as a father.

My confidence, something that had always pulled me through hard times, was gone. The only thing I had was training. Bodybuilding. I trained every day. It was my focus...the only thing that kept me sane. There was no balance in my life. The only semblance of balance was when I would quickly pass it while in the middle of swinging from one pendulum extreme to the next.

Sound familiar? That's the same narrative I used to describe Jess. Somewhere along the way I came to realize that Jess would have wanted me to keep going. Since only one of us made it out...it would not be fair for me to bail on this life. I felt this obligation to stay and–I DON'T FUCKING KNOW (it's something I'm still figuring out). But the fact is I TOOK a life–so my ledger is red–and I don't get to bail out just because I am either lost or can't figure shit out.

I have a responsibility to give some form of reason to this tragedy. To somehow make some sense of it. To that point–If I may–I mentioned it earlier, but allow me to expound a bit. I find it interesting when people tell me, "everything happens for a reason." It makes me really have to wonder...do they actually believe that? I (for one) certainly do not accept–not for a second–that to be a matter of fact. That's a crock of shit...a total cop-out. They then give up all ownership...just throw up their hands and say there's some unknown, mystical reason for shit to happen. Somehow, they are ok with that...even though they may never know the reason? So for some unknown reason you got raped, or your mom starved to death in bed, or you were forced to fire a shot you never wanted to make. And somehow you are good with that? Hmm. FUCK THAT!! I do NOT accept that!! I would offer that if it meant ANYTHING to you, then you wouldn't just give up and accept that shit either!! Life is cold as fuck sometimes, and that's the bottom-line.

The only real way these tragedies will ever make any sense or will ever have any "reason" will be the reason YOU attach to your pain. You want that reason, then give it a fucking reason!! Step the fuck up! Origami that shit!! Meaning this...to actively create something useful from it to help others avoid–or at least to better navigate–more of that same insanity. TAKE THAT TRAGEDY, THAT PAIN...AND GIVE IT A FUCKING REASON!!! Don't just lay down and accept the lie that "everything happens for a reason" That is straight-up bullshit!! OWN THAT SHIT!!! I have come to embrace that concept, I can speak it now. But back then in the aftermath? At that point, I had no idea what to do; and I was still just going through the motions. A shell. I tried to have a relationship, with another physique competitor. We trained together and we worked together, so it should have been a good thing (at least on paper).

It was all wrong though. The same demons I carried before, I still carried; and again, I was involving myself with a person who held their own deep scars and demons. The fact that I was still either waking up screaming and crawling into a corner and crying, or staying up all night rocking on the edge of the bed, was not conducive to a healthy relationship either. It was a train wreck. It is difficult to admit to ourselves... well, it is difficult for me to admit this particular truth. Still, the one common denominator in all of my failed relationships is me. I am the problem.

I love my friends. I value those kindred souls who have stuck around my fucked-up self. As I shared a few chapters of this book (in early form) to them, I would invariably get comments such as, "that's not what I see" or "that's not you anymore" or "I just can't see you that way." Thank God that people can't see your insides like they see your outsides. They can't cut you open and count the rings, seeing the scars of a fire or a dry season. They simply see the snapshot in front of them. This life is a million snapshots. You can't take just one and believe that it represents a total, the sum of who/what a person is or has done.

Now I understand that concept of can apply to both sides of the fence...good and bad. For instance, friends see just what they want to see (cherry picked); whereas, I see all my sins. I am my scars. I would come home for the weekend and drive by my old apartment, but I don't know exactly why. I told my therapist, Dr. Jan, about it. She paused, then said,

"You're reliving it." I would indeed drive by Charlotte street, remembering all the little moments...still seeing her...

Living with your ghost

I saw you today

I smiled

laughed

You were walking down the road

Right in the middle of it

No shoes

Little short jeans skirt

Yelling at the cars

Hair all over

Dirty feet

You didn't care

Not a bit

Not a care in the world

Of course

I know

It wasn't really you

In fact

It couldn't have been you

It was just me

Missing you

Wishing you were still here

It's been years now,

I have thought about you every day

Some days in passing

Some drowning in the memories

I still drive by places we would go

I still see you

In those memories

Laughing

Being you

The you I love and miss so much

And though it hurts

it is also a beautiful thing

That you still exist in those memories

That you are still alive in my heart.

I went to that "BIG" show in Pittsburgh. The one that Jess had wanted so badly to go to. A Big National show–over a thousand competitors–and I won my class. The following year I went again and won a pro-card...dedicating my posing routine to Jessica. That pro-card is considered a big deal in our sport; but for me, every accomplishment...every accolade–shit, my whole life–it was all tainted. The funny thing about life though...life, it don't give a fuck. As long as you are breathing, you are going to get rained on at some point. Some get a light sprinkle, some have a massive storm, and then there's still others who end up with huge hailstones the size of boulders.

I had just found out the woman I had been seeing was cheating on me. I must have had a big "kick me" sign on my ass. Let me just say, I was fairly unimpressed with the drama. I mean think about it...about what I had already endured. A batter swings two bats together simultaneously when he's on deck (warming up), so that it makes the single bat feel like nothing when he's in the batter's box. I had been swinging 6 bats, so this little speed bump was nothing (comparatively).

I was driving back home, licking my wounds, when my ex-wife Lori called. "Brad is in the hospital."

"Oh God, what did he do now?" I shot back with a little chuckle.

She said, "He's in the ER. He's in a coma."

@#$%^&*(?&%! "Wha, What?"

She reiterated, "You heard me, he's in the ER...he wasn't breathing. They are trying to stabilize him now. I came home and found him crumpled on the floor. It looked like he was seizing; there was rocking back and forth, moaning, and foaming at the mouth. There was vomit and piss and shit...it was horrible. I called 911. Please just get here!"

"I...what? I don't understand...What are they saying...? What happened...?"

"They don't know. Tim, you need to hurry."

Tim, you need to hurry... Where had I heard that? You need to hurry....

WAIT!! That's the shit they say in the fucking movies when someone is dying!! My mind was racing while driving eighty down the interstate. My son, the bright spot in my whole fucked up life, the one thing I had a hand in that wasn't a fucked-up mess...

OUT OF THE FUCKING BLUE! Life shows up. Fuck you, life! I walked into the ER. Lori and the rest of the family were there. Almost on cue, the doctor came out of the room where my son was—I only caught a glimpse—but it was enough...like something out of a TV show... tubes, wires, pumps, whirring, and beeping. It was dizzying and surreal. The doctor allowed us to gather then informed us, "Your son has had a brain hemorrhage."

It was like everyone—collectively—had been punched in the stomach. He continued, "but the bleeding is the least of his worries right now. His organs are shutting down. We are doing everything we can."

Deep sighs and crying, but this time something in me was different. I cried every day for a year straight...I was not about to start that shit up again.

CLICK.

"CUT THAT SHIT OUT!! THIS AIN'T DONE, Y'ALL ARE CRYING LIKE THIS IS OVER!! FUCK THAT!!"

I paused to catch my breath...as doctors and nurses stared at me. I looked at Lori, "That is OUR boy in there. This is not even close to being over. He will come out of this!! This is not the time for tears, so y'all stop that shit!!" There she was, paying a visit. That was a Jess moment.

Lori was the first to speak, looking back at me, she said, "You're right...he'll come through it."

I needed to hear that. I was seconds away from breaking down. My anger was a smokescreen for my fear. Lori knew this and really threw me a bone with that line. I went into the room and there he was...my son. There were tubes in his arms, down his throat–I counted 7 pumps connected to him. Helpless...my flesh and blood. I leaned down and whispered in his ear, "You are not allowed to go out like this! You hear me? Get your ass back here from wherever the fuck you are. You are my son. You come from a line of warriors...both grandfathers...your great grandfather. This is not the end for you."

Three days I spent with him in ICU...sleeping on the floor, not eating. Watching as my son would come in and out of the medically induced coma, start fighting and struggling with invisible monsters... unaware, not present...but fighting nonetheless. Saturday morning came, and a nurse with whom I had some serious contention came into check on him. Facetiously I asked if she needed some help, so Nurse Ratchet scowled at me and said she thought she could handle it.

When Brad started waking up again, struggling, fighting the air, she was quickly overwhelmed and asked, "Dad, can you help me?"

Help her. Now she wanted my help, with my shit-eating grin I asked,

"I thought you could handle it, nurse?"

"This is NOT the time for that!!"

Faaack.

She was right. I stood up and started helping to hold him down. His eyes were still blank, still vacant, but as he struggled, something was different...there was a desperation–suddenly, a light came on. I could see it. My son was back. I told the nurse, "He's aware!! He knows we are here this time!!"

She told me to get him to calm down, or she would have to sedate him again.

He was still kicking and fighting, I was trying to talk to him, but panic was in his eyes. My son was scared.

"Brad, Brad, calm down, you're in the hospital."

I was trying to explain, to reason with him, but he had nothing to do with it. Finally, in my big daddy voice, I yelled, "HEY!!! LISTEN TO ME!! YOU STOP THIS SHIT!!!!

He looked at me. Still fighting, I yelled again, "STOP FUCKING FIGHTING OR SHE IS GOING TO KNOCK YOUR ASS OUT AGAIN, AND WE WILL REPEAT IT WHEN YOU WAKE BACK UP, IS THAT WHAT YOU WANT?!?!"

He looked up at me and then, tired of fighting, just slumped back into the bed, resigned to the fact that he would have to follow the rules.

I laughed at his situation, tears of joy streaming down my face, crying with this huge grin on my face. So happy, relieved, after three days.

He went through the nurse's regiment, and they removed the breathing tube. After being told several times not to try and talk the minute the tube came out, he scratched out, "What the fuck happened?"

"Fuck, son, I was hoping you might be able to tell us."

He could not remember a thing. He just woke up in the hospital. There's more to the story, but my real point was simply: Again, life shows up.

A life lost, a life gained, I don't know.

Since Jess, I have been through a whirlwind of events, lost a business, relapse, Jail, lawyers, set-backs, comebacks, a fire; I am still here and somehow, somewhere, along this crazy journey, I feel like I may have reclaimed a piece of my soul. To say such moments are ethereal and fleeting is, at best, understating it. Just accept them as they come, we do the best we can with what is in front of us, that's all you can hope for. We come in, and out, of so many things, nobody has this shit figured out, not one, and if they tell you they do, they are just trying to sell your something.

You get no guarantees. No reprieves. Just because you may have been through some shit doesn't mean there's not more shit coming.

Life is cyclic, so be ready.

You need all those up's and the down's, without them, you end up with a straight line.

The shortest distance between two points.

The Line

Two points in life

Beginning

End

Our journey

Each day

Another step

filled with joy

filled with pain

So many mundane

We celebrate our highs

Trudge through our pain

Putting one foot in front of the other

Truly we cannot exist without both,

We cannot appreciate one without the other.

A Duality.

Without

Ups and downs

Highs and lows

The line of our lives would level

A straight line

the shortest distance between two points

~TD

Just keep moving your feet. That's how it works, you have to stay in motion, that is where our lives exist:

Living Sand

Reflecting on the hourglass

Our lives

2 parts

Past and future

Once past the convergence

Over, done with, gone

Yet before the union

A mystery

Unknown to each of us

the sand that lies ahead

We cannot live in either

Dining on ashes or moments yet to pass

Phantoms, ghosts, or buried

We exist in the movement

In the moment

Passing from one to the next

We exist in the living sand

~TD

This is what saved me. These writings. My catharsis. My quilt, Writing became the fabric. Every piece of my work became a patch, became the very things I stitched in place to continue on, to stay in the game.

Quilt

The fabric of my soul cannot stretch far enough

to mend the hole ripped from my heart

We all have scars

Some deep

Some mere scratches,

then there are the patches.

The patches to cover the holes when the loss is too great

Impossible to mend the tattered ends together

They never heal

The gaps

conspicuous through absence

We must find something to put over them,

To stitch in place

What do we use to cover the gaps in our soul?

Do we become Frankenstein's monster?

An irrelevant patchwork of our pain

Stitched together,

Warped by our loss

Perhaps something more

Pieces discarded

to create something new

Transformed

Greater than the loss

Not the monster

A metamorphosis

A tapestry of growth

Of acceptance

A Quilt.

~TD

I still light a candle for Jessica every year on that anniversary, *3:33am.* I love you, Jessica. Somewhere, someway, we will get it right.

I talk to Annie often... she has been through so much loss. We talk about creating *'The Jessica Foundation.* A not for profit designed to identify and help dual diagnosis women. Fitting, considering the way Jess protected the street girls with whom she ran.

Clan; Family; Kindred SO important. Finding those energies that draw you in, that all gravitate together, I tend to believe that they have always gravitated together.

Accept your friends. Well, everyone. Accept everyone, warts, and all, we all live in a flawed, imperfect world, and we are all flawed, imperfect people.

Share all of you with the people you love and never miss an opportunity to tell them you love them.

Our flaws, our imperfections, the way we find our way through this world. With all of that working against us, against all the odds, THAT is what makes us beautiful.

I, for one, am grateful for that. Some days more than others.

A friend mentioned these last lines from the Great Gatsby that I found it incredibly appropriate: "So we beat on, boats against the current, bourne back ceaselessly into the past."

This is the life we live.

As far as my lobster goes, I miss her, every day, but I do my best to listen to the doctor.

"Don't cry because it's over. Smile because it happened!

- Dr. Suess

Her sly little smile and all.

EPILOGUE

This project was one of the most challenging things I have ever done. I started writing in 2016, 3 years after Jessica's death. It was, at that time, cathartic. I wrote as I said, to purge my mind; to get it out. As I began writing with a purpose, to create this manuscript, it became much darker. At times it was the last thing in the world I wanted to be doing. Dredging it all up, it was painful, horribly so. I would stop for weeks then pick it back up.

I relapsed.

That hurt.

17 years, gone.

To say my arrogance played a part, once again, is understating it.

I have never really developed proper coping skills. I get angry, I throw shit, fight invisible monsters. If that doesn't work, I say fuck it. That is me coping.

An excuse, perhaps (yes), but, in my defense, having never dealt with the trauma, then bringing it all back, reliving it time and time again, already dealing with severe PTSD, I sought an escape. As usual. It worked, briefly, but then I had awakened that fucking demon. I did stay away from my DOC's, you know because that makes it ok (insert big eye-roll here), and yet life continued, it does not let up.

As I said, Brad's condition worsened, developing into Status Epilepticus (look it up).

Work became sketchy for me.

I was arrested and jailed 1,000 miles from home.

I found out I had a daughter.

Lived through a fire, watched helplessly as I lost my sweet dog, Clara.

Remember what I said: LIFE DON'T GIVE A FUCK!!

PLEASE, understand, that's not said as a bad or evil thing. Life is not malicious. It doesn't seek out pain for us any more than it seeks out happiness. It simply is.

You cannot expect the lion not to eat you because you did not eat the lion.

William Blake once said, "The cut worm forgives the plow."

C'est la vie.

There will be more books. I enjoy the process, warts and all.

I am not done here

We all have stories; we all have trials. We all have shit that we wish never would have happened.

But look!! I am still here. You are still here. WE ARE STILL HERE!!

My greatest hope is that we do away with the "right way" to do things. There is no fucking "right way" That is a fucking lie. THAT is the shit that people kill themselves over!

You get punched in the face, you live through it, and you deal with it the best way you can!! No one can tell you how or give you a map. You are a unique individual. Your own mind, your own experiences. You make it through the fire the best possible way, whatever works. Then share, tell somebody: HEY, LOOK, I MADE IT!!

For those who have felt the heat, that will mean the world.

That's what I'm doing.

I am as fucked up as an individual as any person. I am horribly flawed, perfectly imperfect, a complete mess, much like Jessica, a beautiful disaster.

But... HEY!! LOOK, I MADE IT!!

ABOUT THE AUTHOR

Timothy Durning has developed a unique voice through his experiences on a "path less traveled" His stories of success, failure, and tragedy, resonate across a wide section of us, namely, the ordinary, the exiles, the misfits, those of us who come so close only to somehow fall short. His work is raw and unapologetic. Tim has had success in the food industry as a Chef for over 35 years. He has also made strides in the fitness industry, earning an IFBB pro-card and helping others to work toward and do the same. He has seen some incredible highs but has experienced some horribly dark times as well. Somehow, someway, he has made it through, albeit, many times with a lack of grace, yet still stands on the other side to share his experiences, to give reason to the pain, to "Origami that shit" as he would say.

He trusts that life will always show up, at times serendipitously but also, invariably, with the proverbial kick to the face. Tim has seen the rain and has seen that rain fall on us all, so even after the worst that life throws at us, he understands that, life, does indeed, go on.

 facebook.com/tim.durning

 twitter.com/thym43

 amazon.com/author/timothydurning

Made in the USA
Coppell, TX
28 October 2020

40408742R00083